WOMEN RISING

WOMEN RISING

The Journey of Growing Through What We Go Through

2022 LeadHer Publishing

Cover Design - Michelle Fairbanks/Fresh Design
Interior Design - Michelle Fairbanks/Fresh Design

ISBN Print - 978-1-990352-44-7

For more information, visit *www.leadherpublishing.com*
instagram.com/leadherpublishing
or email *hello@leadherpublishing.com*

For more information on the Lead Author, visit *www.theselfcareshop.ca*
instagram.com/the.selfcare.shop or *instagram.com/vickyjomaa*
or email *hello@theselfcareshop.ca*

WOMEN RISING

THE JOURNEY OF GROWING THROUGH WHAT WE GO THROUGH

VICKY JOMAA

AMANDA DIRADDO
ASHLEY TOYE
BRITTANY SCHMIDT
CASSANDRA DEROSA
DANIELLE CHAPUT
DANIELLE PENDLETON
JANET RENNIE
KERRY GIBSON
KRISTA WATSON
MELINDA MELO
MONICA FONSECA
SANDRA WIND

CONTENTS

WHEN THAT
LITTLE VOICE INSIDE
OF YOU STARTS
WHISPERING,
LISTEN TO HER.

VICKY JOMAA

AUTHOR PHOTO: JAMIE CORNISH
INSTAGRAM: @VICKYJOMAA INSTAGRAM | @THE.SELFCARE.SHOP
THESELFCARESHOP.CA

INTRODUCTION

"A woman is the full circle. Within her is the ability to create, nurture, and transform."—Diane Mariechild

Diane Mariechild – thank you for this. Thank you for reminding us that we are creators, nurturers, AND transformers. We are not destined for any one path, outcome, condition, or pattern. We are not defined by our past, experiences, actions, or thought patterns; we are EVOLVED from them.

We women, are strong as fuck.

I should mention now that this is a book full of REAL humans using their REAL voices to express their own stories and experiences. It is raw, unfiltered, and beautifully vulnerable. With that, comes reading about some hard things – some *really* hard things.

Yes, this is a book about women's empowerment. It is a book about stepping into our power and changing patterns, societies, and lives. OUR lives. The lives of those around us. The lives of women, children, and communities that are yet to be created after us. We talk about the lessons learned, the ways in which these experiences can change, shape, and influence us – but no matter what we go through, we continue to grow through it all.

This book talks about all of the hard things that we endure, experience, and expand from. Our journeys are all very different, but they are ALL valid. I invite you to dive into these stories with an open heart, but also with an awareness that some of it may be triggering. If you find yourself experiencing this, know you are safe, seen, and loved. You can always move to the next chapter and come back later, or not. It's up to you. In times of discomfort, sometimes the best thing we can do is lean into it.

In that, lies the ability to grow, learn, and expand.

In this book, that is exactly what these powerful women have done. They have leaned into their experiences, their stories, and their own *knowing* to extract the lessons they've learned, and how they have changed and shaped their lives as a result. Inside the covers of this collection you will find stories about...

MOTHERHOOD
NEURODIVERSITY
HOMELESSNESS
PREGNANCY LOSS & INFERTILITY
ILLNESS & DISEASE
PANDEMICS
GRIEF & LOSS
TRAUMA
MENTAL HEALTH
DISCOVERING OURSELVES

AND SO MUCH MORE.

Oomph. This is all so heavy. But with that, we carry the power to learn, inspire, and create hope.

To learn how to be healthier, happier, and more authentically US.

To inspire those that are still going through, struggling, or navigating some really hard things in their own journeys.

To create hope for a world where we will experience equality, equity, understanding, and universal love without having to fight for it. It will just *be.*

In this book, we hold space for YOU.

Let me tell you a little bit about myself, and how I got to the point of sitting here, writing this introduction for you in this book. (Oh, this book – I have SO much love and hope for you!)

My name is Vicky. I am a wife, mother, small business owner, coffee enthusiast, author, life coach, recoverer of burnout, and ambassador of slow living. Sounds pretty neat when you sum it up in just a few words, but behind those words are years of ebbs and flows, a wide flowing river of continuous soul searching, and MANY lessons learned through all of those seasons of life.

I could add about twelve more titles onto that sentence above to help give you a sense of who I am and what I feel defines me, as I have delved into so many different hobbies, professions, activities, causes, and paths over the years.

My whole life I have felt that I never really "belonged" to any one certain group, club, niche, community, etc. I could never really stay committed to any one activity or *thing* for any length of time. I've been told consistently that I'll never get anywhere if I don't stick it out, tough it out, or continue anyway despite the fact that I very quickly would become bored, unchallenged, and uninspired. I could see my peers, friends, and others around me continuing on with sports, music, and various other things for years while I continued to jump from one activity to the next, only ever sticking with it as long as I needed or wanted to.

I am going somewhere with this. I promise. Hang in there with me.

I divorced my first husband after less than two years of marriage, with a one-year-old baby, at 24 years old.

Shouldn't you try and work it out?

Have you considered getting counselling first?

What about your daughter? Shouldn't you guys try and figure it out for her?

Those are just some of the comments that I got. Let me be real with you; I was not thrilled about a failed marriage at 24 years old with a baby that had me moving back into my parents' house.

But I knew it was the right thing to do. *I KNEW.* I won't list the reasons for you here, because it's irrelevant. This is what I wanted for myself, my daughter, and our future.

Just another thing in Vicky's life that was short lived. (Wait, is my marriage REALLY being compared to the piano lessons that I only did for two years or the time that I thought I wanted to try kickboxing and walked out of the gym before even trying it?)

In retrospect, I am *so fucking proud* of that younger version of me that was able to say no, I don't want to do it anymore. As adults, that is a HARD skill to master, and as women especially, people pleasing and perfectionism can run rampant and interfere with our ability to live authentically and wholly in the way our hearts yearn to. We have been conditioned, trained, and told our entire lives – and for generations before us – to be quiet, keep your place, and do what you're told – but this will NOT be how we continue – we are changing this narrative.

As a result of those really hard decisions I made, I continued on in a post-secondary program that my ex-husband thought was a waste of time and landed my dream job that I worked my ass off for. "Vicky, we did it" I thought to myself. I loved it. I thrived. Like, REALLY THRIVED. And I moved quickly up the ranks, all through which I got married again, had another sweet baby and continued to focus on my career.

Let me tell you, I have never been SO good and SO highly regarded in a position before. I WANTED to stay. I was challenged. I was inspired. I was so good. Everything was falling into place. Maybe this was the thing that I was waiting for. This is the thing that I can stay committed to, and grow with.

I eventually landed in an upper leadership position there and things were going great. They really were. This was my new professional home. *I am staying here for a long time*, I thought to myself.

And I did.

Sigh. Things are always great until they're not so great anymore, amiright? I had it all; I was able to be happily married, a great mom AND have a thriving career. Sounds pretty idealistic from the outside looking in, doesn't it?

But as years passed, the demand started to weigh heavily on me. I had a team at work depending on me, day-in and day-out, and a family at home depending on me, too. I simply did not have the time or energy to also take care of myself. I was not a priority.

I can't let anyone down. I just can't.

But the truth is that I was severely letting myself down by running on autopilot, exhausted, and constantly trying to "keep up."

I had thoughts of feeling like a failing mother because I couldn't attend field trips, lacked the energy at the end of the day to complete simple tasks like home reading, and was often rage-y and short-tempered due to the lack of capacity I had.

I felt like a mediocre wife for not being present when we had the opportunity to be alone and always being too tired to tend to our marriage in the ways I would have liked.

But none of that compared to the feelings I had of being SO FUCKING LOST in my own mind, body and soul. If you have ever felt this way too, I see you.

I cried in silence. A lot. I would take bathroom breaks at work to get a good cry out (quietly), and often found myself with a small pool of tears collecting on my pillow at night, as I replayed all the things and moments that I regretted from the evening with my family.

I should have paid more attention to her tonight (my daughter). I should have wanted to play more with my son.

I *should* have…

I *wish* I had…

These thoughts would often ruminate in my mind and my heart felt heavy. I wasn't the woman, individual, mother, wife, or anything else that I felt I wanted to be.

But I trudged on. I tried desperately to hang onto the career I was so proud of, while also trying my darndest to be the mother, wife, and human outside of that world I wanted to be – which is funny to me now since the definition of insanity is doing the same thing over and over and expecting the result to change. I kept hoping it would change or get better, but it didn't.

Sometimes, life has a way of slapping us in the face to wake us from our trance and open our eyes. For me, that slap was a world pandemic. In what felt like overnight, the world as we knew it was suddenly turned upside down and backwards.

This world event has changed the way we live, work, and think. And I know that a lot of the time, we are just fucking sick of talking about it, but in all fairness, there is a lot to be observed and learned through this experience. For many of us, like myself, this was a catalyst to changing how I lived my life.

As two parents with very demanding careers, we now had two children without childcare and school that were, like all school-aged kids, now at home 24/7.

How in the actual eff are we going to do this!?

We came up with a schedule that rotated in-office and at-home days, and it seemed to work pretty well actually, all things considered with, you know, the fuckery that was the world at the time.

But now, here I was, spending more time at home than I ever had.

We played outside – lots.

I helped them with school – lots.

We laughed – LOTS.

Oh my god… am I having fun AND being present in the moment?!

I felt these small sparks of joy that I hadn't felt in SO FUCKING LONG.

When that little voice inside of you starts whispering, ***listen to her***. She is trying to tell you something that truly, you already know, but she wants you to *acknowledge her.*

I hear you.

I was finally listening to those little voices in my heart and mind. I was paying attention to those body cues that often go unacknowledged…

I hear them all. I FEEL them all now…finally.

Within five months of the start of the pandemic, I told my husband that I was going to quit my job to work on myself, and be more present for our children and our marriage. The rest, I was going to figure out later.

"Let's do it," he said, with zero hesitation. (Not a day goes by that I do not acknowledge and appreciate this human and partner.)

I am almost done with this story, I promise, but I am leading up to a revolutionary moment in my life (another one).

Once pandemic restrictions had lifted a bit, I started finding time to go to the gym again and thought I would try listening to podcasts. This seemed like a pretty popular thing to do so I gave it a shot.

Turns out, I did not like listening to podcasts when I worked out. Not one bit. I personally prefer crime TV or mindless, hilarious sitcoms.

But I digress.

I can't help but believe that I gave it a shot for a reason because one of the ONLY podcasts I listened to from beginning to end was with Brene Brown and Adam Grant, talking about the power of knowing what you don't know. In this episode, they touch on this idea of majoring in curiosity, and being guided by that rather than conviction in order to know what you don't know and want to learn. The idea was to become ***continuously curious***. This concept may have well been shouted from the rooftops with giant red blinking lights and pyrotechnics because it STUCK OUT TO ME in a way that I cannot describe.

I immediately turned to Google because it resonated so deeply with me. I just felt that I was on the cusp of knowing something that I didn't know. It took a bit of digging, but eventually…

Up popped a word that changed my own perception of my life and identity forever. Seriously, it was that profound.

Multipassionate.

To summarize, this essentially means that I have varied interests, passions, and talents that I feel drawn to pursue and utilize, and that the juggling of wearing different hats brings me more joy and happiness than focusing on one thing ever will. It is the very thing that actually makes me fulfilled.

This might be the niche, title, community of people, etc. that really makes me feel like I belong.

This is my superpower, not my downfall.

Through this, I have now embraced the idea that it is OKAY to want to do different things. It is OKAY to follow my heart and not the external pressures of society. It is OKAY to take care of myself so that I can better take care of those around me. It is OKAY to change my mind, bounce from idea to action in many different areas, and pursue a variety of passions.

I wanted to become a life coach, so I did. I wanted to be a better mom and wife, so I made changes that allowed me to do so. I wanted to open an online shop dedicated to women and self-care, so I did.

I wanted to write a book – *so I freaking did that too.*

And here we are. Another book that was sparked from an idea that was the result of all that growing I did through what I had gone through.

My story was about me – finding myself when I had felt completely lost and out of touch. It was about embracing who I was, and how I wanted my life to look and feel. It was about taking that leap of faith and *leaning in.*

My wishes for you in life are much the same, and there are a few things that I want you to know.

We are often made to feel like we need to fix something about ourselves. This is not true. Trust me; you are not broken.

Your characteristics, passions, traits and quirks are uniquely you. They are not your burdens; they are your gifts.

We will be faced with many challenges, situations, and seasons in this life. We have the ability to grow through what we go through. To choose what comes next. **We cannot control everything, but the things we CAN control are far more powerful than the factors we cannot.**

Honestly, I could make a list of a hundred more things, but I am going to let the stories of these next twelve women take the spotlight, and allow their own stories of **rising** fill these pages with words of wisdom and lessons learned. They are truly awe-inspiring and amazing.

So if you are reading this right now, thank you. Thank you for showing up and taking time out of your busy life to walk through this with us. This book is called *Women RISING* for a reason. We are continuously growing, learning, and leaning in as various seasons in our lives are happening before us. Nothing is finite or definitive when it comes to our choices, abilities, desires, and ultimately, our own knowledge and what we can do with it.

The reality is that we are always in-process – continuously flowing through life, in-and-out of different phases of the journey. This is where I am with mine, and my hope for you in this book is that you find solace in knowing that no matter what your journey looks like…

You are not alone.
You are amazing and deserving.
You are seen, heard, and validated.
And you will continue to RISE.

Sending love & light,
Vicky Xo

THE STRUGGLE THAT
YOU ARE FACING TODAY
WAS PUT IN FRONT OF
YOU TO HELP YOU
DEVELOP YOUR STRENGTH
FOR TOMORROW.

AMANDA DIRADDO

AUTHOR PHOTO: LEAH SMITH
INSTAGRAM: @GETTHEKEYWITHAD | DIRADDOREALESTATE.COM

CHAPTER 1

It all started with a phone call that would change my life forever.

It was Tuesday, May 18th, a sunny spring day, and just a typical morning for me. I was at our new listing, taking some photos and videos.

At 11:26 a.m. I got the call from my stepdad, "I just sent your Mom away in an ambulance." My first instinct was that it wasn't anything too serious. She must've just hurt herself or she got too much sun out in the garden.

Little did I know, this was about to turn into the worst day of my life.

Earlier that morning, Mom had called me. She was at the nursery, trying to find us the specific flowers that I wanted to include in our hanging baskets. "They're so fucking expensive. I say we wait and find them somewhere else!" I rushed her off the phone and said "Yeah, yeah, sorry I'm just busy at work, but I'll see you tonight!"

Those were my final words to my Mom.

Shortly after she had called me, she returned home where she and my stepdad were working in the garden. Suddenly she shouted for his help. "My head feels like it's going to explode!" she said, as she held her head.

Because of COVID, they wouldn't let my stepdad ride in the ambulance. She was still coherent when they took off, sharing a final "I love you" with him. The paramedics told him to call her phone in an hour and they'd let him know what to do at that time. When he told me this over the phone, I told him to call immediately!

I got in my car and when he called me back, I could hear the fear in his voice. "They told me to come to the hospital now." I immediately knew something was wrong. You weren't welcomed into a hospital as a visitor during this pandemic unless something was wrong.

Being just five minutes away from the hospital, I headed over there on my own. My husband, Justin, met me there, to find me collapsed in the middle of the parking lot. I had called my Mom's phone, in hopes that she would be the one to answer, but instead I got a nurse. I almost wished I hadn't called or asked what was going on.

When I told her I was in the parking lot, she said she would come out to meet me. As we rushed into the ER entrance together, I looked at her and asked, "is this bad?" She responded, with fear in her eyes, with just one word, "yes"…

I'll never lose the image of my sweet Mom, laying there, helplessly breathing to the beat of the machines. I just kept stroking her pretty blonde hair and telling her everything was going to be okay.

It truly felt like I was on the set of a fucking movie. This couldn't be real.

The rest of our day was filled with a hospital transfer, a couple of surgeries, several shitty phone calls, lots of prayers, and finished off with a sleepless night.

Because of COVID, we couldn't be with Mom. As a family, we spent days in a hospital parking lot, waiting hours and hours for the next phone call update.

You know the feeling of not wanting to ask the necessary questions, because you just don't want the answers? Well a couple days after holding onto hope, our whole world came crashing down.

We were called into a meeting room in the ICU at Toronto Western Hospital, where we met with a wonderful, kind-hearted doctor who had been caring for Mom. With compassion and sadness, he shared the news that no one wants to receive. Mom had suffered a major stroke, and there'd been consistent bleeding in the brain which had caused severe brain damage.

"If this is even survivable, there's a big difference between 'existing' and 'living.' I didn't know your Mom, but I need you to think about what your Mom would want. I understand that you have some very difficult decisions to make as a family."

All I could hear in my head was Mom saying, "if I ever get to being like that, put a fucking bullet in my head." There was no question what needed to be done here, but you still find hope to hold onto, even though it doesn't really exist. She would never want to be remembered as anything but the fun, spunky, party animal, hot blonde that she was.

Only my sister, stepdad, and I had seen Mom that first day and really understood the state that she was in. Without seeing it, it's hard to really grasp what we're truly dealing with. You try to picture what she looks like. What does this really mean? Does she just look like the sleeping beauty that she is? With time, will her fingers start to wiggle and she'll eventually open her eyes?

At 29 years old, this is a decision that you never want to have to make. It's not even something that you can ever imagine having to do.

I think the doctors sat with our family for three or four hours the next day, answering the questions we had been avoiding asking. Being told that your Mom will never walk, talk, eat, or even breathe on her own again – IF she could survive this, that is – is something you can't even fathom. I was with her three days ago, shopping and gardening together.

We finally got to go and see Mom. This was the first time our other siblings and my husband got to see her. I'll never forget the devastation and outpour of tears that they all had as they re-entered the waiting room. I knew what had to be done. Mom would resent us forever if we even thought twice.

For the next few days, we got to visit with her. The staff at the hospital were so wonderful. They encouraged us to have the family and grandchildren write messages on a sheet, which we laid with her for her final days. We surrounded her with family photos and brought a radio so she could relax to the sound of rock and roll.

We'd sit and talk to her, and play videos for her, of her grandbabies laughing and squealing. I know she could hear us and found the strength to hold on for the time she did so that we could be with her and say our goodbyes.

On Sunday, May 23rd, at 6:10 p.m., Mom passed away peacefully surrounded by the people who loved her most. Although we may not have been ready, she was. That night, the sunset lit the sky on fire. And being Victoria Day long weekend, the firework show of a lifetime followed. I knew those were both gifts from Mom – a sign that she was at peace, and as expected, she was going to go out with a bang.

Since I was a young girl, I've always been a mama's girl, glued to my Mom's hip. I didn't know it was possible to love someone or something so much. I just remember how I felt when I looked up at her. I admired her so, so much. My heart was so full and my goal in life was to make my Mom proud. And I'm so glad that I DID!

I was thirteen when my parents divorced. At such a young age, I watched my Mom struggle to leave an unhealthy relationship and question what was best for her and her girls. From the outside looking in, staying would've been the safe decision – a nice house, nice cars, and money wasn't an issue. But I'm so glad that she found the strength within to take that leap of faith. The next several years weren't easy. Mom started her own cleaning business just so she could scrape by and pay the bills. But believe it or not, although we had very little, materially, we three girls grew so much stronger together and found a new kind of happiness. I look back at the shit my Mom went through for us and the pain she must've endured. All she wanted was for her girls to be happy and to feel loved, and that we did.

From that point on, I'd never allow myself to be put into a situation like my Mom was, where I couldn't care for myself or my children, on my own. I committed to working the late bartending shifts, on top of full-time college, in order to pay my own tuition and buy my first car (yes, it was a sexy blue Sunfire!). I truly believe this was the first step to becoming the strong woman and entrepreneur that I am today. This hard work and drive at a young age – it molds you.

At the age of 24, I met the man of my dreams. What started off as a "fun summer fling" quickly turned into *holy shit we're now buying a house and starting our life together!* From the moment I met Justin, I knew he would push me to be the best version of myself, and still, to this day, he continues to do so.

At the age of 25, I was at a standstill and had no idea what the hell I wanted to do or who I wanted to be. Justin pushed me to get my real estate license and from there, I started my career with a BANG, and I haven't looked back since!

After a couple of short years in the business, it was time to spread my wings and soar! At the end of 2019, my husband got his real estate license and the Diraddo Real Estate Team was born. Oh, and did I forget to mention that within that first year of "soaring," my husband quit his job of eight years, I left the team that I had been working with, we found out we were pregnant, AND the COVID-19 pandemic hit? No big deal, right? It's fine. I'm fine (insert a laugh-cry GIF). Reality – we were shitting our pants!

BUT, what were we going to do? We were going to PONY THE FUCK UP – that's what we were going to do! Time to accept the obstacles thrown our way, and carry on with the plan to smash our first year as the dynamic duo! Remember, you only get one opportunity to make a first impression – and THAT is what we were about to do!

Fast-forward to our one-year anniversary as Diraddo Real Estate, and DAMN, did we ever crush it. We grew our brand, sold 48 homes, and earned a Platinum Award from our Brokerage, all while bringing our first baby girl into the world and with this damn pandemic still kicking. I'll never forget uploading a million dollar listing, in between my contractions, and then selling two homes, IN THE HOSPITAL, the day that our daughter was born.

I shit you not, the videos of sweet baby Blake the day she was born, all you can hear is Justin on the phone in the background, pacing back and forth, negotiating deals! Oh, and mat leave? What's mat leave? LOL.

In year two as Diraddo Real Estate, we had a newborn, decided to sell our first home, buy a new home that we needed to totally gut, and move into a small rental in central Oshawa with our baby while we renovated our new home, all while the pandemic was STILL lingering. And on month five of that year, my Mom suddenly passed away and our whole world flipped upside down. Yet we still smashed our goals, sold 73 houses, ranked #7 in all of Keller Williams Canada, achieved the Top Team Award and Double Platinum Award within our Brokerage, and welcomed two amazing additions to our team.

What I'm trying to get at here, is that success isn't just luck. Success is earned by doing things that other people just aren't willing to do. Are you a "play it safe" kind of person, or a "fuck it, let's go for it" kind of person?

Maybe we're given these challenges in life for a reason, not to just run from them. Maybe we hold the decision in our hands. Do we want to grow and rise to the occasion? Or will we merely idle and coast? Maybe we all need to work on shifting our mindset when it comes to things being thrown at us – like a global pandemic, being laid off, or losing a loved one.

Because the reality is, this is life. And what I'm learning is that there's a lot more that is out of our control than we'd like to think. So how can you find resiliency instead of settling for defeat?

What is resiliency?

What is hardship?

What does it look like to overcome your most challenging obstacles?

When I think back to my life two years ago, my greatest challenge didn't even come close to what I've been working through this past year. It's as if life is preparing you, step-by-step, chapter-by-chapter, test-by-test, for another obstacle to overcome. You're building up your strength.

Each obstacle brings you more strength and growth, bringing you closer to being the best version of yourself. As long as you make the decision within, you will grow instead of crumble.

A few weeks had passed since losing Mom. I remember sitting in the car in the driveway with Justin, and he said something that has really stuck with me. He said, "Some people go through an experience like this and grow from it. Some people will let it ruin the rest of their life. You're going to come out of this a better, stronger version of Amanda. I know it."

At that moment, I felt sheer defeat. There was no way I was coming out of this a better person. My life had crumbled. How could I possibly overcome this?

In those first few days, weeks… The thought of "how can I ever get through the next six months, year, 30 years without my best friend?" would side-swipe me, out of nowhere, as if I was driving 100 miles per hour, straight into a brick wall. It felt like my heart was being torn out of my chest in a split second. How suddenly this overwhelming emotion would hit was something I'd never experienced before.

Losing your mother at such a young age, when you've just entered motherhood yourself – is unimaginable. At a time when I've needed her the most, I'm left to figure this out on my own. I'd lie if I said I haven't felt abandoned at times. My motherhood journey was supposed to look so different. All the plans Mom had with her grandbabies and all the memories that were to be made – she would talk about walking my daughter, Blake, to the ice cream store in town this summer. And taking her shopping, and to the zoo.

We've all been robbed…

And as I sit here writing this, our second daughter just turned one week old today! The thought of doing this a second time around without my Mom brought on so many different emotions. Mainly guilt, but also fear, sadness and anger. At a time that's supposed to be so joyful, I felt guilty for harbouring these negative emotions.

When I found out that my due date fell on the same week that Mom had passed, I didn't know how to feel. How was I supposed to celebrate the arrival of my new baby, while also grieving the one-year anniversary of this heart-wrenching loss? But it's all so clear, now that baby Oaklee has arrived. I truly believe Mom sent us this blessing. Call it divine intervention, if you will. Even though Mom can't be here physically, she still finds ways to bring us the joy and happiness that she wants us to experience. The sense of comfort and love that baby Oaklee has brought me is like no other. I truly believe that a piece of Mom was brought back to me with my baby girl. I know that she is still with me and supporting me through this journey, just in a different way.

Since I experienced this loss, I've turned to spirituality to help with healing and connecting. I'm learning to open up to the signs we receive and the feeling of our loved ones around us. And it has brought such a sense of peace and balance back into my life.

Reiki healing and connecting with Mom through mediumship have been two major outlets for me on this journey. Not only am I receiving signs and messages, but I also feel the presence of Mom's bright, loving personality come through when I'm practicing these things. It's a beautiful feeling that just can't be described.

Another huge outlet for me is talking about my journey – the good, the bad, and the ugly. This has helped me immensely. Whether it's writing in my journal, sharing my thoughts through a post on social media, speaking to a therapist or… WRITING A BOOK (say what?!). Releasing my feelings and thoughts, from up in my head and heart, and onto paper or my social page, gives me a sense of freedom.

And a bonus that I've learned along the way, is that it's also helping others around me, which is so uplifting.

Now don't get me wrong, I'm far from "fixed." This will be something that I chip away at for the rest of my life. I know I'll never stop missing her and having moments where grief hits me like a transport truck, but I'm learning how to embrace those waves and allow them to come and go.

There are always going to be really shitty days – sometimes even shitty weeks – where getting out of bed and doing life seems impossible. I still have them, and I expect to face them for a very long time. But trusting the signs from Mom and the universe has really helped me change the way that I look at the cards that I've been dealt. It gives me a sense of knowing that Mom is still with me, and often, closer than she ever was before.

It's unfortunate that grief never goes away, because it hurts so bad, but there's also beauty in that.

"You will lose someone you can't live without, and your heart will be badly broken, and the bad news is that you will never completely get over the loss of your beloved. But this is also the good news. They live forever in your broken heart that doesn't seal back up. And you come through. It's like having a broken leg that never heals perfectly – that still hurts when the weather gets cold, but you learn to dance with the limp." - Anne Lamott

I feel that I'm not only carrying grief for myself, but I'm carrying it for her as well. It was not her time to go. There was still so much to experience and so much love and joy to be shared. She earned that and deserved that. But in that, I've learned to find joy in the little things in life – like the feeling of the sun beating on my face, the crisp breeze blowing through my hair, or watching the clouds glide through the sky – the beautiful things in life that we don't take the time to appreciate as much as we should. Because one day, the beautiful things that surround us will all be taken away, and the Pinterest-worthy home and the perfectly manicured lawn won't matter anymore. What goes with you are the memories you made, the love that was shared, and the person you were able to become while you were here on Earth.

So if there are dark demons in your life, it's time to figure out a way to face and embrace them.

Instead of feeling like *why is this happening to me?* Instead, think *how can I learn from this and come out the other side a better person?* Those roadblocks don't have to stop you from living. Look at them as an opportunity to persevere.

What do you want to achieve in this life? What does your heart and soul truly desire?

How can you find more balance in your life, making time to be present for the things that matter most? Because let me remind you, you aren't promised tomorrow. You aren't promised next week, or next year.

How do you want to be remembered?

People say "everything happens for a reason." I can't wrap my head around a reason that my Mom was taken from us, but I knew I needed to find one. A reason to push forward. I can't change what has happened, but what I can do is create a reason to carry on and grow from it. That's what she would want and that is what I deserve.

When I really reflect on my 30 years, surrounded by the love I was gifted, I feel so blessed. I also understand why this loss feels like my heart has been ripped from my body.

A childhood friend said to me, "I hope you find comfort knowing that you grieve intensely because you loved intensely. A bond and love like that is forever, no matter what."

The greater the love, the greater the loss.

I've been taught how to love with all of my heart. That is my goal as a mother, wife, friend, sister and daughter. The people that I love deserve to feel the love that I was gifted. And although I may have taken it for granted at the time, it is now so clear to me how unique and rare that type of love is. I will be forever grateful that I was lucky enough to experience it for as long as I did, because many people won't experience it in their lifetime.

If you're feeling like you're at a roadblock and wondering how or if you'll ever get back to "normal" – know that the answer lies deep within you. While this may be your "new normal" – know that it can be better than the old. This is your opportunity to rise above and grow. You're stronger than you think.

So ask yourself: "What is it that can help me find strength and bring me peace?"

A year ago I couldn't go two minutes without falling to my knees and sobbing uncontrollably. I remember a few months back, I caught myself singing and dancing in the mirror and it totally caught me off-guard.

Now, every day, I crank up the tunes and dance, sing, and smile in the car with my daughter! Six months ago I was unsure if I'd ever do those things again.

While the heartache of missing my Mom still trickles in often, I can confidently say that the really good days outweigh the bad ones. I'm back to enjoying the things that I love, and am now focused, more than ever, on living a life that I'm proud of – spending time with, and focusing on, the people and things that matter the most!

I often forget to reflect on all of my victories, both small and large, and just how far I've come!

Something I've asked myself is: *What do I want people to think when they look at me?* I know there's always going to be a new chapter to the "Amanda story" – the girl who lost her Mom at 29 years old – but I won't let that define me.

Instead, how about having people look at me as that badass Mom and successful business owner, who's LIVING and OVERCAME SOME DIFFICULT SHIT!? I want to be an inspiration to others – living a life that I deserve, that I've earned, and that I know my Mom would want me to live for me and my family.

Instead of feeling sorry for yourself, look deep within and find the strength to empower yourself and those around you.

So I challenge you… How can you flip the script?

MAKE THE CHOICE
TO RISE ABOVE
WHATEVER YOUR
SITUATION IS AND FIND
HAPPINESS IN IT.

ASHLEY TOYE

INSTAGRAM: @ASHLEYPANTRY
WWW.ASHLEYPANTRY.COM

CHAPTER 2

At a very young age, it was clear that my view of the world was different and that I was "unique," a word that has been used to describe me for as long as I can remember. It took a couple of decades for me to realize who I really was, and why my thoughts and surroundings ended up hijacking my livelihood. For so many years, I hid and buried my pain and traumas because the struggles of everyone else seemed far more important. In my mind, the people, relationships and difficult experiences that I attracted were a side effect of an incurable mental defect. As a result, living and caring for others before myself made the most sense. Life was about protecting others from pain and heartache – filling their cups and leaving mine empty. As I've lived my life uncontrollably walking in everyone else's shoes and concealing my struggles, it's time to share more about the shoes I've been wearing – the shoes of an empath.

The term "empath" comes from the word empathy, which is the ability to understand and experience the feelings of others outside of your own perspective. As an empath, it's an entirely different level of sensing and experiencing emotions (both pain and happiness), as if they were your own. This means picking up on everything from subtle and emotional cues to traumas – absorbing them like a sponge and having no ability to jump out. The compassion fatigue from internalizing and not knowing how to shut it off can start to change your hardwiring.

After ages of distressing patterns, my uncontrollable empathy almost killed my soul and overall well-being. It became normal to regularly assault myself with negative thought patterns and behaviors, and eventually this vicious cycle left me feeling apologetic for my existence. I was drowning in empathy, and my body and brain had enough. After years of trying to climb out from a dark hole, a shocking tragedy occurred, and it nearly ended me.

As a young girl, I felt a heaviness that would follow me into the classroom, activities, and many normal day-to-day moments. Being in the presence of other people would cause emotional highs and lows that never made any sense to me. My escape from this heaviness would be using my creativity and imagination to come up with a way to place myself into another fantasy world – a world of fun, laughter, and innocence. I was the queen of make believe, imaginary characters, and humor. It was difficult *not* to be overly compassionate, nurturing, and peacemaking. I was always tuned in to the emotions and energies of people – processing, solving scenarios in my head, and coming up with strategies or ways to ensure others were free from distress and heartache. There was a constant desire to bring joy and comfort to others. When my senses told me what they were feeling, I'd give them what they needed.

Witnessing anything traumatic (on television or in person) would cause deep emotional disturbances – some of these experiences would cause night terrors, or end up haunting me for years. I would feel for the characters or victims on the news as if it were someone I knew. So much time was spent in my own head – thinking, brainstorming, interpreting, and analyzing others and what they were going through.

My dreams were always so vivid, detailed, and often stressful. If I shared details with others about what I was going through, it quickly validated that I wasn't "normal." The negative commentary from my sibling and peers reinforced my internal beliefs. Hearing remarks about being weird and unattractive crushed me, but I knew better than to let it show. Keeping my head down, and mirroring others to blend into society seemed like the best approach to avoid being a target for shame and bullying. Having heightened awareness of my surroundings allowed me to protect myself by finding the safe places where I could actually be myself. I did my best to fly under the radar and avoid any spotlight, conflict, or trouble, meanwhile always discreetly working behind the scenes to protect others from harm.

It was never enjoyable to be in large crowds for extended periods. Disneyland, for instance, was an unusual experience. The park was filled with crowds, lineups, and sounds – children screaming or crying, people getting off rides looking ill. The flood of happy and fearful emotions surrounding me overpowered my ability to enjoy myself. I wanted to like it, but there was too much to process. My favourite ride turned out to be the floating tea cups – the water, calm and quiet, and the people surrounding me were content. The most pleasant and vivid memory I had was in the evening – the rides and chaos ended, and my mom took me to watch the Disney parade. She let me pick out a stuffed animal in the giftshop. I remember hugging that Minnie Mouse so tightly, as I sat next to her and watched the floats go by. The enjoyment that I felt rarely matched how others experienced things.

Although I did everything in my power to play it cool, I often felt defected, and like a complete outsider. Why was I able to read people, and absorb their pain and suffering? Why was I so bothered when I witnessed suffering that wasn't even mine – bullying, loss, abuse? I would take it all on. I knew deep down that I wasn't unintelligent, but the constant distractions of emotions inhibited my concentration, decreased my ability to learn, and hindered my confidence. I couldn't absorb classroom instruction and often would take my notes and books home to teach myself when I wasn't distracted with my brain trying to compute and absorb the dozens of emotions that surrounded me. The fantasies and dreams about someone else were stronger and more frequent – I craved the mental break and distraction from my thought patterns. There were dozens of nights when I would worry so much about other people and things, I would start to shake for hours and get sick to my stomach. My concerned parents struggled to understand these intense episodes, and for me it felt impossible to interpret.

I would do everything in my power to avoid the spotlight. Silently achieving and reaching personal milestones was way more comfortable than bragging. I always downplayed myself. Aside from the bullies and narcissists, seeing others shine bright was fulfilling. I always felt for the underdogs and would cheer them on, while putting myself last. Happiness was felt when other people were at peace – acknowledging quiet or suffering classmates and doing subtle things to bring them joy felt right. People would often ask me to help mediate, solve problems, and it almost seemed like second nature for me to advocate for others, or to be there to bail them out of a negative situation. Being on the sidelines was preferred, especially when it came to team sports. I never wanted to hurt people, and team sports felt too aggressive and risky. Solo sports were my calling and a healthier outlet because it was way less mentally taxing.

Growing into adolescence and early adulthood brought more patterns to the surface. My anxiety was heightened, and my mind struggled to be at peace. Letting myself go was rare, and confined spaces and routines would make me feel very claustrophobic. I would feel aggravated if I couldn't have my own space to regroup from energies. Although cognisant of my differences, it was never a thought to dig deeper into it.

Decisions (especially the big ones) were always hard for me because they were centered around what was best for everyone else. I always needed time and space to try and sort out my thoughts and worries. My decision to be a nutritionist and attend university in the United States felt like the best next step after high school. To make this happen, it required studying hard, practicing tennis as much as possible, and working three jobs to save money.

When awarded a tennis scholarship, I felt one step closer to happiness and contentment. In my mind, the perfect formula to a joyful life was education, career, marriage, and children. Checking these boxes meant that one day this success would bring me my "golden ticket," a visualization I came up with as a child. Holding onto this belief and fantasizing about it gave me hope for the future – that the mental torment would be relieved one day.

This dream of being successful and content made me want to work hard to achieve, even if it meant putting in all of those extra hours behind the scenes. Being overly aware of my surroundings meant that I could observe how my peers went down the wrong paths, and I knew exactly who and what to stay away from. Subconsciously, I did everything I could to live my life in a healthy way and avoid unnecessary conflict – there was no room for drugs, skipping school, or being reckless if I wanted that golden ticket.

My dreams were always visualizations of me serving and helping others, and inspiring them to be healthier. University was a transition, but at the same time it felt like a breath of fresh air.

I was on my way to entering that happy colorful adult chapter, and was convinced that I was well on my way to squashing the defective traits from my past life.

I kept trying to focus on the fun, and experiences, and conquering the challenges of university life; however those defects and patterns started reappearing. I would get mad at myself for not having more energy to submerge myself in constant social functions or highly populated situations. At night, especially, my anxiety and worry for others seemed to get worse and cause me not to sleep. I would do what everyone else did – watch a tv show, read a novel – only to find myself dreaming about what I watched or read and waking up in a sweaty or stressful state. I was caught in a vicious exhausting cycle, but I did my best to ignore and carry on with my ridiculously busy schedule of traveling on tennis trips, studying, working, and maintaining friendships. The light I felt like I was trying so hard to reach started to fade again.

I found myself getting caught in exhausting and toxic traps, while trying to heal and nurture everyone around me. I knew I had great empathy for people, but I didn't realize the level that it was affecting me. In an attempt to break free from the darkness that was appearing, I wanted to try something new by breaking down my walls and allowing myself to come out of my shell more and trust others. Being alone was much easier for me, and I didn't understand why I was left so physically and emotionally exhausted being around others. I chose to ignore it, and I decided to go all in.

Everything started to shift when I fully devoted my heart and soul into romantic relationships.

Although unclear at the time, there were definite patterns with each of these relationships – lying, cheating, narcissistic personality traits, and repeated second chances. Over and over, I would excuse their bad behavior because I could feel the pain they operated from. I had compassion toward their weaknesses, insecurities, and mistakes.

I fully invested myself in a relationship and was convinced this person was my forever. He was the opposite of me – loud, confident, outgoing, and self-centered. He made me feel alive, and for that reason I chose to ignore his reputation. The good I saw in him was something I wanted so badly to be true; however it all came crashing down when he chose to cheat. How I found out and how he did it humiliated me and left me heartsick. Everyone knew. His apology and remorseful acts were convincing, and my empathy for him overpowered my ability to walk away. I stuffed my hurt down and gave him another chance, only to be left with the same outcome. When I didn't accept him back, the anger and aggression started to appear. I struggled to permanently detach myself from him and end the relationship, as losing him and removing him from my life felt unbearable. I felt even more defective, and blamed myself for not being "better" so that he wouldn't want to cheat. The pain of it all made me feel lost and insecure – I started to lose more respect for myself.

I tried to carry on. Other men would use and take advantage of me and my kindness without consequence. I felt such pain, yet I would let the feelings and wants of others surpass my needs. When a stranger sexually assaulted me, I decided not to pursue charges because "it could have been worse." At the time, I convinced myself that my need for justice was almost selfish – other victims needed the system more than me. I started to hit the books even harder and do everything I could to excel at things that were in my control. Physical fitness became an outlet, and my evenings were spent behind closed doors studying and making sense of what was taught in the classroom. After walking across the stage and graduating with honors, I moved to Texas to start my first nutrition job. I accepted full responsibility for every bit of pain and heartache I experienced, but refused to let my mistakes sink me.

The next relationship was with a man who pulled on my heartstrings so much that it seemed impossible to turn my back. He was recently widowed, highly intelligent, motivated, and had more of a "good guy" vibe. Immediately, the damage and pain of his experiences took over my body and brain. With enough care, support, and understanding, my mind told me I could love him back to life. No matter how much time passed, he remained involved with his deceased wife's life, and he would hide me from her family and friends. Being surrounded by her pictures and belongings was challenging, but my compassion took over. When my feelings were disregarded, the red flags became stronger. When the situation wasn't improving, I expressed concerns, and this triggered him to pull out his gun and threaten his life. After I wrestled the gun out of his hands, I was horrified, and realized there would be no easy way out of this. I chose to bury my concerns, focus on the positives, and move forward.

We started fresh and relocated to a different city in Texas. An opportunity arose for me to do what I always dreamed – to work for myself as a nutritionist and start my own business. I felt perhaps this new collaborative career path with my partner would connect and strengthen our relationship. Since I didn't have any permanent status in the United States, a job change meant that I needed to visit the U.S./Canada border to apply for a new work visa.

I arrived at that border alone and damaged, but determined and ready to have my golden ticket breakthrough moment. I didn't want to inconvenience my partner or anyone else, so I chose to transport my 25-year-old self to the U.S. land border from Texas, and enter the port of entry with my application documents.

When I was called into the office that evening, my gut told me right away that something was wrong. There were over ten sets of eyes on me, all men, and I was alone. Everything about their eyes, demean-

or, and body language was off. I felt it in every bone of my body – this wasn't like the other times. What should have been a simple ten minute process escalated to an unimaginable and appalling overnight interrogation. Within the first few hours I tried my best to keep my composure. I did *everything* I was told. I let them search me, humiliate me, rip my belongings apart, take my phone, share my personal photos with one another, make offensive comments, and treat me like a piece of rotten scum. The only offense under my belt was a traffic violation, yet I was being treated like I was a criminal with a lifelong record. It was like my night terrors coming to fruition in a blink of an eye, and there was no waking up from it. These narcissistic border "protection" guards abused their power with such pleasure, over and over, all night long.

When there was no trace of drugs or crime, they started to question my intentions of applying for a new work visa. After their relentless digging and overstepping, they managed to fin d a crack in my paperwork and ran with it. I was mentally tortured, violated, and physically threatened to the point where the "good cop" pulled me aside and said that I should do what I am told to do, or brutal harm would result.

There were two choices given to me: sign a paper agreeing to a 5-year ban from the U.S., or get shipped to a mental institution. When I pleaded for them to release me without either, they slammed a chain in front of me and stated that they were going to wrap it around me and drag me to the back wall and essentially do whatever they wanted to do. They were in charge and I was powerless. The stress, lack of rest and nourishment, combined with the manipulative interrogation techniques ended up getting the best of me. I just wanted it to stop, and this meant "confessing" and surrendering to something I didn't do. With no hope in sight, my signature was signed on that paper. It seemed like the best and only option to free myself, and the "good cop" convinced me that the chances of an immediate appeal were high, and returning to my life was within reach. I believed him, obeyed, and returned to Canada.

My world shattered into pieces. The light I was chasing completely disappeared. From doing my best to thrive independently, to being trapped in my home country and living under my parents roof was a very drastic change. There was so much hate and punishment toward myself for not preparing properly, or doing things differently in the application process. The devastation I felt combined with the sadness of my family and friends was torturous. I was equipped and experienced other people's emotions and traumas, but being in the victim hotseat and having people try to "fix" me and show sympathy felt catastrophic. People who knew were appalled at what happened to me – they wanted justice for me and media involvement to warn others. At that moment in time, my only desire was to hide under a rock and go back to my previous life. Even though it wasn't perfect, it was much better than taking a million steps backward.

After learning that signing that paper was the worst thing I could have done in that scenario, the feelings of guilt, shame, and blame grew even stronger. Choosing the mental institution would have been a better option, and the "why didn't I do__," started to haunt and flood my thoughts. The border guards covered their tracks and nothing on paper was in my favor. Other stories were brought to my attention about border guards abusing their power, but not one compared to the severity of mine. My self-hate increased and the fight in me faded.

For a girl always trying to walk a straight, narrow, and humble path, this was an excruciatingly painful experience. One that was kept very private, and that still remains a struggle to talk about.

Burdening others with my problems was just too painful. It felt like I was mourning my own death while taking on the heartbreak and sadness of the loved ones surrounding me. I'd let everyone down in every direction. Viewing myself as "damaged goods," was already ingrained in me, and having this horrific trauma added to the pile only solidified my lifelong belief of inadequacy. I was drowning in hopelessness.

For years, I'd been silently beat down (absorbing my own anguish and punishing myself for it), while experiencing the endless emotional contagion of everyone else's pain and suffering. Not one person knew about my compounded secret past baggage and traumas. In this hidden PTSD state, it felt like I was dragging myself through the mud with oversized baggage that just wouldn't stop multiplying.

Starting over again, I relocated to Alberta and did everything possible to fly under the radar and avoid burdening anyone with my situation. The only part of my U.S. life that was left was my boyfriend – and I was not ready to let him go. My mind told me that the weight of the incident was so strong that his past wrongdoings no longer mattered.

For over a year, a lot of effort was put in on my end to maintain the relationship, but the reciprocation started to fade. After days of silence, he called to say he'd found another woman. In his final remarks he disclosed that every piece of furniture and all of my personal belongings had been thrown away. He made this cruel decision without any warning and had the upper hand to screw me over. It was another crushing blow that magnified how helpless I was. My friendships, relationships, and assets were lost. My life blew up and my possessions may as well have burned in a fire (only there was no insurance policy to recoup any of the loss). It was financially crippling and devastating to lose irreplaceable pictures and keepsakes. This had gone too far, and my desire to continue living started to fade.

Everything with my physical and mental health was declining rapidly. Coping with this resulted in self-medicating, self-sabotaging, and inflicting more pain to punish myself. I would drag my feet all day just to look forward to the moment I could go to sleep and escape it all – only to have a "rest" of vivid nightmares at night. It was rare to sleep without an anxiety attack or flashback. The only thing that fueled me was serving others and ensuring they were content. I would continuously attempt to rebuild myself, my career, and go through the motions of this life that was nothing of what I had dreamed and fantasized about.

The miniscule amount of energy inside of me was devoted to my nutrition clients and loved ones – counseling and preparing meals while trying to meet everyone's needs. Even though my nervous system was shot and my thoughts were harsh, it kept me alive. The light I spent years fighting for felt flameless, and my only hope was to live to serve others.

After my five-year sentence had passed, I grew the courage to face the terrorizing border issue, with the optimistic hope of having the option to visit the U.S. again. Upon my arrival, my hope was taken away.

The officer on shift was in disbelief and apologetic when he read my documents and looked into my case. He informed me that the border guards misled me into believing the ban was for five years – it was documented in their system as a lifetime ban.

My heart sank, and so did my soul, as the horror, shame, and embarrassment resurfaced. Those five years had already felt like a lifetime – and now this game of gaslighting, manipulation, threatening and torturing was going to haunt me until my death.

I did everything in my power to try and heal myself, but the decline of my physical and mental health was happening far too fast. I was in and out of doctors offices, emergency rooms, therapist appointments and PTSD recovery groups, while drowning in fatigue. The time and effort to try and get myself out of this hole was exhausting. I was hooked up to various pieces of medical equipment and had brain scans and MRI's, while being diagnosed with an autoimmune disease, adrenal fatigue, and fibromyalgia. The treatments hardly made a dent in my suffering, and the root of my struggles was never addressed. After a difficult loss occurred due to a medical malpractice incident, my faith in the system helping me diminished.

The next few years were spent in a new relationship with a man who fooled me into thinking I was his number one. At the very start of our relationship, he hid me from his ex and convinced me it was to "protect" her from feeling bad. A couple of years later, it turned out he never ended the communication with her and strung her along with intimate conversations and photos. My senses told me he was keeping her on the back burner, but I chose to disregard my gut feelings and gave him a pass. With the strain of my health and emotional issues, my mind told me accepting this was a fair deal.

Over a year later, I accidentally stumbled upon his hidden porn addiction. After confronting him, the severity and long duration of this addiction was revealed. I was shocked, mortified, and felt disgusting, inadequate, and alone. My empathy kicked in and my compassion allowed me to hyper-focus on his good qualities. Attempting to help him get help was a losing battle. Instead, the "I can fix myself without a professional" attitude was thrown at me. I tried his way for a very long time, while silently feeling inadequate and disgusting. Shortly after accepting his marriage proposal, a major shift happened. It took the impeccable timing of a good friend's words (and a few moments in the mirror) to listen to my senses and acknowledge the path I was taking.

I decided to do my own self-discovery and get a different kind of help from a very wise and intuitive woman. Within minutes, my routine past trauma/relationship speech was interrupted and she said, "you're an empath and here are some resources and tests I need you to take." What she said was taken with a grain of salt, and my eyes rolled. After being mislabeled and misdiagnosed my entire life, the word was dismissed until my own research could prove it.

After scoring high on the tests and investigating the materials, my eyes started to cautiously open. It felt overwhelming and annoying, especially after noticing how much online bullies and trolls liked to target empaths (as if it was made up). I took some space from the resources and just started to pay attention and observe myself and my thoughts more. Things started to make sense, too much sense. It was enough to reignite that light in me, and start to fight for myself again. This time, the fight seemed worth it because it made so much sense, and the tools actually fit me. Now that I recognized how, what, and why things unfolded and felt the way they did for me, it was time to take a stab at breaking those unhealthy patterns. For over 30 years, I lived a life not truly knowing why I experienced things the way that I did and felt the way I did. My tank always empty, yet I felt so compelled to give anything that remained to everyone else. Now I knew why.

For the first time in my life, I made a big disrupting decision that wasn't about keeping everyone else content and happy. It was time to fight for my life, and maybe it wasn't too late for that golden ticket to contentment. The choice to cause an emotional eruption in so many people's lives (while in the early stages of breaking patterns) was the biggest and hardest decision. I still hadn't figured out how to effectively deal with who I was, but there was no time to ease into it. Even though I'd been burned so many times in that relationship, the thought of ending things and hurting/losing so many people was a very tough pill to swallow. It caused a major upset – the judgment and backlash combined with the grief and heartache was grueling. Things were worse before they were better, but the biggest reward came when everything started to settle.

Although I *knew* better than to stick around in these relationships, it became automatic to put zero value on my needs. The ultra compassionate feelings toward their weaknesses, insecurities, and mistakes dominated. The pain, worry, and ripple effects of initiating a breakup would cause more anxiety and worry than it was worth. Since getting to the bottom of my own issues seemed useless, it made the most sense to pour my energy into situations that would actually improve. My "fixing" would work, and the progress felt like a glimpse of achievement. I couldn't help but want to continue to support and see them grow. Hyperfocusing on my faults was a way to reassure myself that I wasn't deserving of more. My heightened awareness of being indifferent combined with my deep empathetic qualities continued to cloud my judgement and perspective.

I naturally went about my life compartmentalizing my own tragedy and suffering, while carrying the burden of everyone else's struggles. When faced with trauma, there was nothing in my toolbox. Being an empath and attempting to survive trauma is like tuning into multiple radio stations at once while a bomb is going off. What was already a horrific experience for any person to go through manifested into a pit of extreme darkness. This lack of self-awareness led me on a path that could have had a lot less pain and suffering. It was standard to voluntarily take the blame, even for things that weren't my fault. As an empath, it's normal to feel like you should be an on-call multi-service to others while completely losing track of your own emotions, because you are feeling those of everyone else. As a result, I coped poorly, made mistakes, and lost my voice and confidence. Silently taking punches from others while hiding and beating myself up for my faults was everyday life. In this state, it felt impossible to fight for justice.

It's even harder when you're told that life "should" be fine for you when everything is sound on paper – a scholarship athlete, loving family, honors student, bachelors and masters degree, a career as a nutritionist… I "should" have been healthy, happy, and successful, yet experiences like Disneyland were *difficult.* When you don't have the same fulfillment that others do from certain experiences or activities, it's easy to question yourself. My inability to cope with the trauma as an empath sucked me into an even darker hole of hopelessness. My self worth was lower than low, and this allowed me to believe that I deserved to be matched with painful experiences and relationships. Having no awareness of this extrasensory perception caused me to feel like a complete alien and misfit in society.

As a woman, especially, this became a very dangerous situation in relationships and abusive scenarios. Acts of kindness and extending myself to others without anything in return became my currency. Receiving, however, has always been hard for me, as my inner voice would remind me that doing things alone without any support was punishment for my stupidity and mistakes.

For a big portion of my life, not understanding my "defects" severely affected my confidence and ability to thrive. Accepting myself for what this is hasn't been easy and it's still a process. I'm happy to say that I'm no longer a doormat when it comes to relationships and people in my circle. In the last few years, I've been tested by many people and situations, and chose to discard some toxic energies and self-absorbed people. I've also gained some absolute gems.

The challenges are continuous, however it's getting much easier to navigate. My intuition is a gift that I've learned to use wisely and to listen to. The vulnerability to emotional contagions (similar to "catching" a cold) will always be natural, but it is becoming easier to control. Absorbing the emotions like a magnet from *everyone* in my circle (even a stranger in the grocery store) is possible to manage; it just needs to be filtered properly.

Today, I am very happily married to a man who accepts me, genuinely cares for me, and has the patience to learn more about how I am. We are very different people, but we respect one another, value communication, and continue to grow as a team. He understands my need for space and solitude and tries his best to help me cope with any unexpected triggers. Additionally, he's encouraged me to fight for myself and freedom, and we've recently reopened the border case. I am also eternally grateful for my parents who have been rocks of support in my healing journey.

As an empath, it is so important to acknowledge triggers and establish boundaries. We can't handle "normal" things the way the majority of others do. Reading the news, being in large crowds, or watching a frightening TV show can have undesirable consequences. Protecting and shielding is so important, and I've learned to distance myself from exhausting or negative people and energies. I had to make some shifts in my career, and set strict limits with social media and the people I follow.

Some individuals will have no problem using manipulative tactics to keep you around, while using all of your energy and resources. These narcissists and energy vampires will make you feel like you are useful – using convincing apologies to make you feel valued – but at the same time, they have no problem using you. It's important to be aware of this and to pay attention to who is in your circle and how they treat you. Family members and close friends are no exception. We often allow those who are closest to us hurt us the most. For empaths, this emotional manipulation can be abusive and debilitating to the nervous system.

I've learned that that trauma doesn't need to be suffered in complete silence, and that standing up for my rights is not a burden. It was not necessary to pile the pain of others onto my plate while I was rotting and suffering. I failed to report assault, abuse from men, medical malpractice, and abuse of a weapon. I chose to hide under a rock instead of creating noise around an incident that was wrong. Recognizing the patterns and obtaining the resources to learn strategies to cope and heal is so critical.

This label is not a badge of honor; it's part of my identity that I now work with and not against. The energy and time put into others is carefully chosen and given to those who reciprocate. Volunteering my time, energy, and skills is no longer an everyday offering. Expanding my toolbox to conquer future challenges is a continuous and vital part of my journey. My lack of self-awareness took me on a deeper, more distressing path that damaged my brain and body. The repair work is a daily practice of nourishment, grounding, recharging, quiet time (especially in the morning) and a consistent routine of exercise. Creating recipes and playing with nutritious food is my main healthy outlet for my overactive and innovative brain. The desire to heal others, give, and extend myself will always remain a part of me, but it's done within reason now.

As an empath, taking is much harder than giving, and it's damn hard *not* doing things for others. These gestures are genuinely natural, and have nothing to do with earning brownie points. Learning where to devote that energy, and where it needs to be limited, is all part of the healing process. When you find yourself falling back, there's a podcast or book for that! Please contact me for more information on my healing tools and personal resources.

If used wisely, empathy can play an important role in our lives. Understanding others brings brightness and more functionality to the planet. Highly empathetic people deserve to be loved, and there is a valuable place for them in society. When they step into their powerful shoes, great things can happen in the world.

BRITTANY SCHMIDT

AUTHOR PHOTO: MARIANGELICA FORERO | HONEST HUSTLE
INSTAGRAM: @SPRINKLE.THAT.SPARKLE
@BRITTANYSCHMIDTREALESTATETEAM
WWW.SPRINKLETHATSPARKLE.CA | WWW.BRITTANYSCHMIDT.CA

CHAPTER 3

You Get To Choose

Hi, my name is Brittany Schmidt. I am an entrepreneur who has risen through loads of limiting beliefs, sexual trauma, an eating disorder, pregnancy loss, pre-cancer, and the loss of my mother (who was my best friend).

I have risen up through all of my hardships and leaned into my intuition. I live my soul's calling by embracing my gifts as a psychic medium and spiritual mentor, helping wonderful souls manifest their dream homes as a Real Estate Agent by day, and guiding my Spiritual community toward their hopes and desires by night. I am a successful business owner, wife and mother, and grief thriver. My passion project "Sprinkle That Sparkle" has become a beloved side business that encourages my soul family to lean into their intuition, self-awareness, and to manifest their dream lives using the Sprinkle Affirmation and Journal Prompt Deck and Reflection journal that I created.

I am here to show you that anything you put your mind to is possible for you.

Let's get started –

Once upon a time in a far-off place… nah I'm just kidding. This happened in Kitchener, Ontario probably not too far from where you are reading this. Or, if it is far, I'm so glad that you're here and reading from a distance. My hope for you after reading this chapter is to feel inspired and as though you are capable of absolutely anything despite what the world throws your way.

Of the many lessons that I've learned throughout the course of my journey, the main lesson that I take with me through each chapter of my own book of life is that I am capable of anything that I put my mind to, so long as I believe it to be true.

Let's start from the beginning. You're a little girl or boy. You're told your whole life that you have to be good, proper, have good manners, and you have to do what society expects of you. There's very little room to actually just be who you are in existence.

Fortunately for me, I grew up in a household where my parents were quite comfortable allowing me to be who I was. I'm an only child, and I think that really allowed me to be the trailblazer for my family in many ways because I didn't have anybody else setting an example or an expectation of what being a child should look like.

My mother came from a very broken household where she felt trapped. Her parents had given her away to a very religious aunt and grandmother. My father grew up in a household with parents who focus very much on the way that things appear to the outside world, often buying into societal norms. Both of them, like myself, never really felt like they fit in anywhere 100%.

Like my intuitive parents before me, I've known since I was a small child that I had gifts that were unexplainable. I've known when the weather will change, when certain events will take place, how people are feeling before they open their mouth to explain it, and who they are at the core of their being. I've often predicted the future for myself and others – including family members' passings. There have also been times that I would take a different route, knowing that there was trouble that lay ahead or removing myself from situations before things came forward that were dangerous.

As a child, I was told that spending my recesses hugging trees was a strange way to be and I was bullied. After a while, a lot of the limiting beliefs and opinions that were placed on me by others started to sink in. Being empathic as a child is amazing but also problematic because you're constantly told what you should or shouldn't be doing or feeling. I have always felt ALL THE THINGS! It's overwhelming, especially with parents who didn't understand the sensitivity (or perhaps feared it). This was no fault of their own; they just didn't understand it.

As a teen, I worked in a restaurant. In that restaurant, it was very much take the orders, do the job, don't question things. Naturally, I never felt as if I fit in there, despite loving interacting with people and connecting with them on a regular basis. I was basically told to sit down, shut up, and do the work.

In my later years, when I moved into the corporate world, I very much felt a similar sense of don't ask questions and move along with whatever you're told. Don't mess with the status quo. While working for that financial institution, I often found that when I would come up with new ideas, my ideas would be stolen by people in leadership positions and played off as their own – and met with quite a bit of positive feedback. I found this frustrating after a while because I always felt that those who came up with the idea should be recognized for them. This resulted in bitterness sinking in.

I had grown through the ranks of the corporate world to a position of team lead and had many times put myself out there and gotten interviewed to become a manager with hopes that I could lead change on a larger scale. What I was told time and time again was that I would not be chosen as a manager until I received a degree of some sort. I was hurt by this; I was already doing the job. I was simply asking to be paid for. This concept absolutely blows my mind because I know there are many people out in this world who make tons of money and are extremely abundant. They have a wealth of knowledge and ideas, and do not have a university or college education. In my opinion, for the role I was in, it was not needed. With all of the limiting beliefs swirling around me, I felt that maybe I should get a college or university degree. I doubted myself and felt incredibly uncomfortable. I realized quickly that the only purpose it would serve was to benefit me in rising up the ranks. If the people I was working for couldn't see the value that I brought to the table, was this really the right place for me to be working?

If you get nothing else from this chapter, I hope that you never allow someone else's opinion of you – of what you have or don't have – to determine how you view yourself or limit what you're able to accomplish. You are capable of doing anything with or without a college education (unless you want to become a professional that requires the accreditation, of course). There are some things that life experience cannot replace.

This brings me to my next place in my journey where huge realizations and growth took place for me. Do you know in life when people say that there's a defining moment? The moment for me was May 26, 2013. My husband and I got engaged in 2012 after moving into our new home in 2011. We were so excited by what our future could hold as newly engaged young people, the potential adventures were endless.

Little did we know, our lives would be shattered by the event that took place at our Buck and Doe. To set the stage and circle back to what I mentioned earlier about having an inner knowing, the week prior to our Buck and Doe, I met with a colleague and told him that I feared that someone close to me was going to passaway. I hoped that it wouldn't be my husband-to-be because I was so excited about what our future together would be like.

Okay, now back to May 25, 2013. It's early in the morning. My husband and I went to garage sales for new items for our house. As we are driving home, we drive down the road that my parents live on.

I felt called to stop, despite it being seven o'clock in the morning and knowing that my mom slept in on Saturdays and my dad would likely be asleep on the couch where he often fell asleep after watching TV.

We knocked on the door and stepped inside. Surprisingly, both of my parents were awake. My Mom was super excited to see us and we ended up staying for breakfast and talking with them for a couple hours.

From there, my husband went back home and I took off to get my hair and make-up trial done. I spent the day being pampered, enjoying and reveling in the idea that I would soon be a married woman and celebrating with our friends and family that evening.

We got ready at home and were delighted with anticipation. One of our friends picked us up, and we were off! It was being held in the old New Hamburg arena, which has two levels. When we got there, we were met with T-shirts with our names and faces of each other on them from when we were awkward kids. We chatted with our family before the guests started to arrive and had an absolute blast. There are pictures of my mom behind me the entire evening as we walked around. She walked me around showing off all of the things that she had contributed to the night.

Everyone was having the time of their lives, which included drinking, having fun, kibitzing around – it was absolutely wonderful. We played games including hula-hoops and tons of dancing. I think all of the activity is part of the reason the night took a turn.

Around eleven o'clock, I saw my dad sitting outside of the bathroom on a single chair. I approached him and asked what was going on. He said my mom wasn't feeling well and that she was in the bathroom feeling sick. I walked into the bathroom and one of her friends was holding the door to the handicap stall. Concerned, I opened the door to find my mom vomiting. She mentioned having had diarrhea and looked very unwell. The look on her face and the color of her skin is something that still haunts me to this day.

I offered multiple times to call an ambulance to which she denied just saying that she wasn't feeling well and it must've been something she ate. My dad was also not feeling well earlier that day and they had eaten at a new restaurant, so we assumed maybe they had gotten food poisoning.

I asked her if she'd like me to clean her up and get her ready to go home. She agreed. We tied her hair back in a scrunchy. I got her a bucket and a bottle of water, and we tidied her up and got her ready to go outside. My dad took her arm and was helping her down the stairs. I remember standing at the top of the staircase. I yelled, "Mom! I love you! Call me when you get home."

I had a sinking feeling in my stomach that I would never hear from my mom again. I ignored my intuition, and went back to the party.

Moments later, my dad came flying up the stairs with a look of absolute terror on his face. He said that my mom had had a stroke and that she was outside in the ambulance. The look in his eyes told another story. I raced down to see what was going on. The fire trucks and ambulance were already there. It turns out that the ambulance in our small town had been out on a call that didn't turn out to be anything. It was down the road and able to get there quickly.

Luckily, we had a police officer who was acting as a bouncer for our Buck and Doe. He had been helping my dad perform CPR on my mom for a period of time before the ambulance got there. I remember banging on the back of the ambulance asking them to let me in as they defibrillated my mom trying to bring her back to life. Her body kept bouncing up on the table. She had passed away in the car right before my Dad's eyes. We were fortunate that she was resuscitated and brought to the hospital and able to have heart surgery.

I remember holding her hand in the emergency room as the people around me talked about their weekend and what their plans were. I looked up and there was a pregnant nurse standing in the doorway looking absolutely horrified by the fact that I was there holding my Mom's hand while she was taking what we would soon find out to be some of her last breaths. I kept talking to her and thought I saw her heart monitor pick up each time I whispered how much I loved her into her ear.

She was carried off to prepare for surgery and as they did so, I remember the doctor saying, "Looks like I won't be sleeping in the next 24 hours." I wonder how long this surgeon had been awake at this point. I made my way to the bathroom and found a woman that was clearly struggling with a drug addiction in the bathroom scratching at her skin sitting up on the countertop. I asked if I could help her. In hindsight it seems so odd to me that I would ask this person if I could help them when I was in a moment of needing help myself, yet my empathetic self really struggled to see this woman battling addiction.

Around seven o'clock the next morning, they came out into the waiting room where we were sleeping in piles as some of the wedding party had stayed with us while others cleaned up after the Buck and Doe. The doctor told us to go home as my mom was put on ice packs to bring the swelling down after all of the CPR that had taken place in her heart surgery.

When we walked out of the hospital, I felt that I would probably never see my mom again, yet we did as we were instructed. Dave and I went home and had a nap. I woke up at 10:30 and went to call my dad – and he was already on the other line calling me. It had been confirmed that my mom had passed away. When we arrived at the hospital, I fell into the arms of the nurse who opened the ICU door.

Years later, when I was asked to help sell a property for a family who had lost a loved one, that same nurse sat in front of me. She was the mother of someone I went to high school with, and the story came full-circle. I was able to help her family with a transition just as she had helped me. The next couple of weeks after Mom's passing were an absolute blur. I remember helping my dad with all of the arrangements and getting all of her financial things sorted out. What was supposed to be a happy time in my life, turned into a traumatic experience. While working through all of the things that needed to be done, I forgot to give myself space to grieve.

I truly believe that my mom had the time of her life that night. It was her farewell party as well as our Buck and Doe. As I lay here writing this in my hammock, I'm reminded of how fucking lucky I was to have somebody in my life who was my best friend and also my mother. Please heed this as a reminder to hold those that are dear to you close. Life is so fucking precious, and we have no idea when it can be taken away from us.

I don't want you to live in a place of fear. I want you to live in a place of gratitude for those you cherish and remain present in the moment. There were so many things I had planned for us that simply never came to be. My biggest regret was not taking enough pictures or being fully present with my Mom. I wish for five minutes that I could be with her and tell her how much I care and how amazing she was. I still do so in Spirit and am fortunate that she continues to guide me from the great beyond, but a hug from her on a hard day would go a long way, or even just her loving guidance.

After the weeks of constant attention surrounding my Mom's passing, the true levels of grief hit HARD. People weren't checking in on me as often. They had moved on with their lives and I felt ALONE. What nobody tells you about grief is that it's such a funny bitch. Some days you feel perfectly fine, and you have moments of joy. Other days it comes crashing in like a giant wave or a tsunami that you're struck by, and you land flat on your ass. What I've come to realize is that there's no right or wrong way to grieve. Life isn't linear and death isn't either.

I remember sitting on my porch looking out into the world and watching everyone else go about their day as if nothing was wrong, as I was sitting in a place of deep despair. "I was once like you," I thought to myself, bitter at the fact that others weren't suffering the way I was, despite never wishing the acute grief I was feeling on anyone.

There is nothing anybody could say, do, or give me that would make me feel any other way than the cloud of darkness that had bestowed itself upon me. At the moment I didn't realize that what was the worst possible thing that could've happened in my life, would also end up being the biggest blessing.

Here are some of the lessons that my mom's death has taught me that I feel called to share:

1) *Life is precious. Live it to your absolute fullest.*
2) *Never allow anyone's expectations or thoughts about you to dictate how you feel about yourself.*
3) *Life doesn't have to be difficult; we make it that way.*
4) *Your mind is your greatest ally or worst enemy; you get to choose.*
5) *Just be. Be present. Be you. Be, do, say whatever the fuck you want!*

6) *Take vacations.*

7) *Live how you want, not according to the expectations of others.*

8) *Do the things – whatever it is that lights you up – DO IT!*

9) *The only consistency in life is that it's inconsistent.*

10) *Nothing is guaranteed so take the chances.*

11) *Be your own best friend; there is NOBODY else more qualified.*

12) *Healthy boundaries are imperative to your mental health, including boundaries with yourself.*

13) *Less is more. Simplicity is magic.*

14) *Make music to the beat of your own drum. Your authenticity is the most beautiful thing that you bring to this world.*

15) *Work through your traumas, heal the wounds, understand your limiting beliefs, and be willing to do the work to integrate them into your growth.*

We create limitations in our minds of what we are capable of doing based on societal pressure, limiting beliefs bestowed upon us by those before us, and/or with stories that we create in our minds of how things should be. What would happen if you would just surrender to what it is? When someone in your life passes away, you have to surrender to what it is. There's no choice. There is no option, no take backs, no Mulligan, no redo. You have a choice to move on in a way that's constructive, or you can stay stuck in that perpetual state of grief – which likely doesn't serve your highest and best good. Lean into the hard feelings. Feel them. Remind yourself of the good times. Talk about the experience, and be open with your healing. Do whatever the fuck feels good to you in the moment if that is what it takes you get you through. Piece by piece and day by day, you have the choice to continue to rebuild your new life without the person you are missing – or to remain sad.

The thing about grief is that there is also a lot of guilt, but the deceased loved one would tell you that guilt doesn't serve you. They would want you to be happy and live your life to the very fullest no matter what that looks like for you. It took a very long time for me to come to the space of acceptance of my mom's death.

There are still days, almost ten years later, that I sit in disbelief that I have created a successful business, became a wife, raised two daughters, and had tons of life experience without her by my side. After she passed away, I felt as if I had a makeover of my mind, body, and soul. My core values shifted dramatically. What I mean by that is the rules that applied prior to her passing no longer existed. This rule that I had to stay in my corporate job in order to obtain wealth and have security didn't exist. Security doesn't exist because something that you deem to be secure can be taken from you in an instant. Her passing was proof of that. I decided that if I was going to be a betting woman, which we are each and every day, I was going to bet on myself.

My mother was a realtor, and my father is a realtor. I've always enjoyed connecting with people, and being in and out of houses my entire life, I felt a pull to look into following in their footsteps. I sold my first house when I was three years old simply by asking the people my parents were showing the house to whether or not they liked it. They answered yes, and I told them they should buy it – and so they did.

After my mother's passing, my husband and I got married in September 2013, and I got pregnant almost immediately. When my first daughter was born, I decided that I would go back to work for one year and decide what I wanted to do. At this point, I started taking self-led courses to become a real estate agent and really did a deep dive into how I wanted my ideal life to look.

B was one year old, and I was heading back to work when we got pregnant with C. I went back to work pregnant, with the understanding that I would go back again for one full year and slowly get the word out of what I was doing. B had health issues with constant ear infections so while navigating that and consistent morning sickness, I knew that once C was born, it was going to be very difficult for me to obtain my license while still working full-time with two little kids.

I was in a position where I could start selling, but in order to continue selling, I had to obtain the remainder of the courses. I had gone back to work in January of 2017 after giving birth to our second and by July, I sold my first house, an employee of the same company I worked for, whom I met while getting pedicures when we were both pregnant. I am so grateful that she took a chance on me.

Around December of that year, I had sold a few houses and knew that I was never ever going to look back. I WAS HOOKED. The thrill of being such an integral part in helping others better their lives was something that I had always craved in the corporate world. This new role scratched the itch that I didn't know was that deep.

I decided to give my notice because it had been close to a year since my youngest daughter was born, and I found out that the co-team lead that I had been working with was also going to give his notice as he was moving to another team. I decided to stay on for an additional three months to help with the transition, train the new leaders so my team wasn't left high and dry, and also obtain my bonus so that I put myself in a better financial position.

What I will say to you now may shock you. Despite making almost a $10,000 bonus, what I realized is that if I had spent that time and energy working in my business, I probably would have achieved twice that had I invested my time and energy into the Real Estate business that I was excited and passionate about. Some food for thought here is that while you think you're doing yourself a favor in this place of "security" in a role that you're not lit up about, you may actually be taking away from something that you could be growing for yourself.

In my first full year of real estate, I helped 16 clients. 16 people trusted me enough to help them buy or sell a HOME, the most sacred thing that people own. I am still in awe to this day of the feeling that I get when I am able to help aligned clients. That meant that I had earned three times what my original salary was despite not having any benefits or pension. When I went back to Sun Life to have a conversation with my previous leader, he asked how many houses I had sold and when I told him, I could see that he was calculating in his head how much money I had earned. He had always been so worried about the numbers and service levels. It worked for him but that environment of focusing on transactions instead of interaction no longer fit the bill of the life that I was looking to create.

He asked if I was ever coming back because there was an unspoken energy that I brought to the team that he didn't quite have an understanding of before I left. I inspired people and people inspired me. There is nothing more magical than the synergy of a cohesive group working together toward one common goal. There is nothing more deflating than working in a space where they don't allow you to bring that to the table despite knowing it's for the greater good of the business. I explained that I was never coming back because I was living in my soul's purpose at this point.

Since then, I've grown my business to be a multi-six-figure business despite having gone through trauma as a young adult, despite having been brought up with limiting beliefs and societal pressures, despite being WEIRD my whole life and never fitting in, and despite not having a college or university education in the formal sense outside of my required course.

Here's what I do have, and I bet you do too:

PASSION
EXCITEMENT
FREEDOM
LOVE
CONNECTION
DESIRE
FUN
CHALLENGES
CHOICE
ALIGNED CLIENTS
CONFIDENCE IN MYSELF
TRUST IN MY INTUITION
MY DREAM LIFE
EMPATHY

I've learned to lean into the gifts that I had as a little girl but didn't feel comfortable enough to do anything with. I am a psychic medium and Reiki practitioner who also has the pleasure of helping others heal.

I do this through tapping into my intuition to share guidance with others on where they can take steps in aligned action within their life to put themselves back on the right path if they've gone slightly awry. Naturally this helps me with my Real Estate clients as well!

I've brought to life an affirmation and reflection journal now being sold on Amazon. I've also created self-love and awareness cards to help with manifestation. There are affirmations on the front, and journal prompts on the back to help with self-love – all because of the trials and tribulations I've been through in grief and other trauma experienced over the years.

I've risen from a place of darkness, and I feel excited about where this life will lead me.

Remember, the only difference between me and anyone else who has not achieved their dreams yet, is that I truly believe that I can. I chose to see the good that came from the grief. I chose to wake up every day and try again despite how terrible I felt in the moment. I choose to transmute the negative energy that the traumatic experiences brought forward in my life, and I choose to give the goodness in my life my all. I will not be defined by what others think of me. I will not be defined by the stories that I tell myself in moments of weakness. I will not be defined by the grief that I still experience to this day. I get to create the definitions of who I am and nobody else has the honor of doing that for me. You have this power, too. Never forget that.

Anything you grow through, you can glow through.

When I was little, my Dad taught me that if I was struggling, to stand in front of the mirror and yell my name as loud as I could until I believed that I was capable of anything. I encourage you to try that the next time that you are struggling with believing in yourself.

Stand tall in front of your mirror and say the following:

"I am ________ (insert your badass name here) I am special. I am deserving simply for being me. I am an exceptional human being. I'm a beautiful person living a wonderful life. I have been through tough times and they do not define me. Here I stand, ready to live my very best life! I call in all that is for my highest and best good and release anything that no longer serves me."

The last piece of advice that I will leave you with is this. Whenever you have limiting beliefs that creep in, ask yourself these questions:

Is there any evidence that this is not possible for me?

Is there evidence that this is possible for me?

Is there a chance that the stories that I told myself are just stories and not the truth?

Any of the limiting beliefs that you have can be flipped into limitless possibilities. Use me as your proof that your dream life is possible for you because if I can do it, ANYONE can.

Search for the good and live a life of gratitude. There's plenty to be thankful for if you look for it!

Sending you all the love as you navigate your journey through this wonderful thing we call LIFE!

CASSANDRA DEROSA

AUTHOR PHOTO: CASSANDRA DEROSA PHOTOGRAPHY
INSTAGRAM: @CASSDEROSAPHOTO
CASSANDRADEROSAPHOTOGRAPHY.FORMAT.COM

CHAPTER 4

Hi everyone, my name is Cassandra, and I'm joining the other women rising in this awesome co-author project. I have re-written this intro like eight times and I honestly have no idea how else to start it so this is gonna have to do. Haha. I'm a 33-year-old mom of three, wife, and business owner from Alberta, Canada. I wanted to be part of this book to tell my story for a bit of therapy and release, but I'm also here so more women know that they're not alone. There are safe spaces for them inside other women's stories to relate to, find comfort in, and maybe even share their stories one day.

I know now that my story isn't so unique that I am alone in the experiences that I have grown through, but throughout my life I didn't have examples or women sharing similar experiences. It wasn't a story that I had come across until it was put in front of me. I'm hoping that the woman who needs to read this story, is reading this book right now, and this is the moment that she comes across the thing that makes her feel seen, heard, and validated. This chapter is dedicated to that woman – all those women – and is also dedicated to the little girl inside of me who wishes she knew what she knows about herself now.

So on to my story. Here we go.

Have you ever felt so damn alone inside your brain that it scares you? Trapped in a body and brain with such a strong disconnect that you feel like you don't make sense, and constantly feeling like you are just missing a key piece of information?

If that's you too, I'm sorry.

For as long as I can remember, I have ALWAYS felt like I was missing something – missing a key piece of information to help me feel "normal" inside my brain and body. I felt like everyone around me was living in a way that I could not. I could never quite understand how the people around me lived in the same world that I did. While it kept spinning and moving, they lived in it like it wasn't overwhelming, loud, and terrifying.

I was learning as much as I could to ease the massive feelings that I felt, but no matter what I learned, I came out feeling like I couldn't possibly figure out what I needed to know to fit in and feel safe. I really wasn't sure how I "should" be thinking or feeling at any given moment because the overwhelm inside of my head took up so much space that I was lost. I couldn't seem to put the pieces together to live a "normal" life.

Everything had a big feeling, and from the way that kids and adults acted around me, I was producing the "wrong" kind of feelings and reactions to spaces I navigated and the environment I was in. So what did I naturally internalize? I was a weird kid.

Throughout my childhood and adolescence, I was diagnosed with a plethora of different mental health issues to try and explain this "brain mess" as I navigated the cluster of confusing dialogue in my head and feelings in my body. When I was very little, I had an MRI for self harm during tantrums, night terrors every time I slept, and digestive issues. The doctor said I was healthy and it was behavioural.

As I got older, I was diagnosed at eight years old with ADHD. By the time I was an adult, I was diagnosed with everything from Generalized Anxiety to Anxiety & Depressive Disorder. I began to hate going to the doctor. No matter what I seemed to say, or get diagnosed with, I was dismissed and "healthy."

On a daily basis I felt so paralyzed by fear and overwhelm that I restricted my daily life so much. I restricted how and when I left the house, what I did, my friends, and most intensely – my food.

By the time I was 19, I barely did anything aside from going to work, cheer, and coming home. I didn't want to have my boyfriend around all the time or overnight anymore. I spent way less time with friends. I was so trapped by my thoughts that I isolated myself as much as I could without breaking up with my partner, quitting my job, or leaving my sport.

Looking back, the hardest part of living in my body and brain was that nobody outside of me really knew what was going on! I was so lonely and so scared. My friends and family only knew the small small part I allowed them to know. I thought if I told them the truth – the real thoughts and feelings – that they would for sure have me committed, or worse: they would leave me.

From age 19 on, the feelings, fears, and anxiety really ebbed and flowed. Sometimes I would feel relatively "normal" (normal for me, anyway – and honestly what I mean by "normal" is that I still had all of my anxieties and quirks, but I could function a bit more efficiently than when I was overrun by them). Other times I would be paralyzed again as the fears and feelings intensified. The problem was that I never knew what happened to make the better times better, and the worse times worse.

Sometimes I did notice that it was worse in the darker months, so when I mentioned it to my therapist at the time, I got another diagnosis: SAD. Seasonal Affective Disorder is definitely real and to a certain extent I think that it affects me, but because I still had some serious issues in the summer too, I know that wasn't all that was going on.

I continued to do research and Dr. Google became a place of refuge (but also a place of fear). I tried everything that I could think of to try and rid myself of the panic, thoughts, and subsequent feelings that plagued me. I went to therapy, I tried tapping, I tried journalling, different healthy diets, I tried going to the cheer gym more (living through all this I was also a competitive cheerleader, held a full time job, and had a boyfriend who is now my husband of 11 years – so to the outside world, I looked relatively normal). But no matter what, the weird feelings and fears stayed. They weren't always the same, but some common themes stuck with me no matter what.

As the years went on, I only had a couple different regular 9-5 jobs, both of them pretty long term that I held steady. I got engaged and married. I had three children one after the other, two years apart. I appeared to be a "normal" woman in her 20s, living a good life, taking care of her kids.

I kept everything scary inside of my brain, and was determined to function "normally." Meanwhile, the waves of my mental health kept calming and crashing. But by this time – even in the "calm" times – I felt like I was near drowning inside. I continued to seek therapy and I continued to pursue different avenues of physical health to try and lessen the crashing and to find the key to healing myself, all while also caring for my three babies, starting businesses, and trying to keep my relationship together.

By the time my son was three in February of 2020, I was so overwhelmed and so tired of fighting that I started to feel like I didn't want my life anymore. And worse than that, I didn't want to be alive anymore.

I struggled so badly that I really thought that I didn't want to be a mom anymore. Or a wife. Or even a human. I just wanted to go to sleep, be as peaceful as I could, and never wake up. I broke down and I told my mom and my husband how I was feeling.

My mom and my husband called the hotline you're supposed to call when someone you know is having suicidal ideation, and they came to my house and checked on me and the kids for three days in a row. It was so humiliating. I felt like a failure. Like I wasn't doing enough to figure my shit out and I was still no closer to the care I needed or to understanding what was going on inside my body. It still felt like it was all me. A flaw in my abilities.

I constantly felt ill, overwhelmed, anxious, irritable and angry. I was having regular outbursts at my kids, and I had so many sensory issues that my brain and body could not connect or help me find calm.

I started reading self help books, still thinking it was a personality flaw. I was hardly eating but what I did eat was super healthy. I studied nutrition and acted my way through my life as if I was fine to the outside world. (I was far, far from it.) I projected an image of what I WANTED my life to be like. What I HOPED one day it would be. I thought maybe if I pretended hard enough, it would come true. Throughout this acting I was majorly depressed. I spent most of my time in bed, and I did exactly enough to make sure that my kids' basic needs were met, but not much more. My business fell apart; I didn't care about it anymore. On top of everything there was a global pandemic. I just resigned myself to feeling this way forever, even though what I showed the world was much different. Hope was losing its glimmer, and I didn't think I would make it to 40.

Then I met a friend that changed my life forever. Our kids were getting close before we were at the time, as we lived across the street from each other, so when the pandemic hit our relationship grew because we decided to become cohorts for our kiddos so they had some friends to play with. She may not know it, but she was the catalyst to me starting to heal and get better.

One summer day, we were sitting in her yard watching our kids play, and I told her the things in my head. I don't know why she felt so safe. Maybe it was because she herself was a therapist, or because her kindness leaked out of her pores and I felt validated by simply being in her presence.

I'll never forget the moment that she ran upstairs, got her DSM-5, went through some questions with me, and said, "You don't have just anxiety. It sounds to me like you have OCD." I was so confused. I thought OCD was all washing your hands (which honestly, I did) and flicking light switches and turning door knobs. I had no idea that it was so much more broad. I was instantly overwhelmed, but something felt different. I had a lead. I had a pathway.

I called my mom first and I talked to her. She said along with ADHD, the doctor told her at age 8 I also had "OCD tendencies." WHAT? So this was known? How did I miss this?

I started seeing a therapist that specialized in OCD soon after. While seeing her, and learning more about this disorder than I ever had, I also learned I had what's called ARFID (avoidant restrictive food intake disorder) and in a complete plot twist, she told me she thought that WHY I had multiple different diagnoses is because I may be on the autism spectrum. This would encompass and explain all of the diagnoses, sensory issues, etc.

The interesting thing about this is that my sister was recently diagnosed at the time, and we had had a discussion about her diagnosis, and I remember thinking to myself *I feel some of those ways, too, but I can't possibly be autistic*. I then listed off all of the reasons in my head why I wasn't based on preconceived notions that I had about what autistic people were like.

So when I completed the tests that my therapist gave me and scored as an autistic individual would, I was kind of shocked. I felt wrong – like I was stealing a label that wasn't mine. So what did I do? Yep. More friggen "research" on myself and what this might mean.

The more research I did, the more that diagnosis fit. The more things I read and learned from other autistic women, the more I cried. The more I learned, the more the noise started to fall away and things snapped together like someone handed me the key to what I was missing. The more things that clicked and the more things started to make sense, it's as if this huge weight was being pulled off my shoulders. This wasn't my fault. ALL of this wasn't because I had a lack of willpower, or because I wasn't smart enough or trying hard enough, it was because I was autistic. The more I became aware of what truly was going on with me and how my brain worked, the more I started to feel a little bit better. For the first time in my life, I felt seen.

Don't get me wrong – I am still an autistic person with OCD, ARFID, sensory issues, three kids, a business, and all of the things that come with life as a mother, wife and business owner. So this shit is still hard, and all of the pain and trauma didn't magically disappear, but I feel...

more aware and more calm. I have more compassion toward myself. I have an answer and it's not all my fault. Yes I am weird, now I know why I'm weird – and maybe it's not so bad to be weird.

Over the large time period of all my struggles, I was still trying to be what I perceived as a "normal" person in a world not designed for me, instead of asking for or taking the accommodations that I needed. I didn't really know how to advocate for what I needed – hell, I didn't even know what I needed! I am still learning about the world, being an autistic woman and a mom in this world, developing my core values, and settling into my authentic self.

Here's the thing, though – when I learned these new things about myself, this process of advocacy started to expedite itself. The last year in particular has been so incredibly transformative for me. I reopened a business I closed in the height of my struggle. I became a certified yoga teacher. I learned how to care for myself and monitor my needs like I have never done before. I have learned to say no when I wanna say no, and ask for space when I need it. I have completely stopped pursuing friendships with women (or people in general) who make me feel like shit or like I am not good enough, or don't show interest in maintaining a friendship with me at all. I have advocated for change in my marriage and help from my husband more than ever. My husband also finally understood why I am the way I am, and found refuge and healing in it.

I also sought more knowledge about parenting as an autistic person, and I have recognized the signs that my oldest daughter is likely also on the spectrum (along with the help of my beautiful sister who recognized some traits in myself and her a long while ago). I am learning how to meet her needs. I can openly communicate with my kids with what is happening inside of me, and they are compassionate to my sensory needs. It has made parenting and being understanding so much easier. I can speak to my own inner child a bit better, too, as I learn to understand what my children need from a new lens.

Most importantly, though, I am learning who I REALLY am underneath ALL of the things that I learned from what other people did to be accepted. And you know what's awesome? Not giving one single fuck about what I look like to others. I'm trying my best to give myself radical self-acceptance and self-love. It was the recognition that through all that I went through, and what I currently was going through, that my feelings and needs were and are valid and my value never changed. That realization woke me up to all of the things that I needed to do to keep myself feeling confident and capable more of the time.

Once I started to really SEE me – not as one big mess, but as a good human who deserved to live authentically no matter what society told me or how I was conditioned to feel – better days started to come.

So why did I decide to share it here? Because for 30 years I kept my inner monologue to myself, afraid of what it would mean to speak my fears, thoughts, and even my desires out loud. I was so afraid of my weirdness and so afraid of admitting what it was like to be me. I held it all in and it nearly killed me.

So now I wanna speak it! Hell, I wanna scream it. I know that the hiding and self-isolation did nothing but make me feel so much worse, so there must be women out there, right now, doing the same thing that I did, who need me to share this so they can start to release and feel relief.

For me, releasing the stigma of mental health diagnoses, releasing the shame associated with needing help, and embracing my need for accommodations, compassion, love, and care from my partner, and friendships, my environment, and myself – is what made everything less heavy. Dropping my mask, owning my weirdness, and being authentically myself everywhere I felt physically safe to do so was and still is absolutely crucial in my continual healing process. I stopped doing things that I don't like. I let myself be awkward and weird. I made new friends who love me for my weirdness and I left circles where I had to change to fit in.

I decided that my physical and mental health were a priority. I needed to take care of myself and set some strict boundaries with others when it came to what kind of energy and ideals I allowed to enter my bubble of peace. I take more space and make more time for the things that I love and the people I love – one of those people, being me!

I covet and protect my alone time. This is something that every woman should do. MOMS – I'm looking at you, too. At first you are GOING to feel like a bitch for saying no, and telling your loved ones to give you space, but I promise you, it's only because of the garbage that you have internalized your whole life about everyone else but you needing to be your first priority like your kids, husband, friends, family – BLAH BLAH BLAH – but that is just the MOST untrue. You cannot be what you need to be for the people that need you if your needs are going unmet. This doesn't mean that you have to ignore the needs of your dependents. It just means that you need to prioritize and ADD yourself to that list of dependents, and ask for help.

A woman's value is often placed on her service to others and how she shows up for others in her life. But love, your value is innate. Intrinsic. Enormous. You are IMPORTANT. You are the only you, and you are special. You deserve to be a priority and to be cared for. You deserve to be on the schedule, front of mind, and loved by yourself – as you are right now. You don't need to change yourself in any way to deserve this kind of self-love, advocacy for your needs, compassion, and self-care. You cannot hate yourself or hide yourself into a better or happier version of yourself. The love and care needs to start now.

I'm here to reclaim a part of me that was lost as I tell my story. I'm here to share my imperfection in this world of smoke and mirrors, with people only showing you what they want to show. (I should know; I did it too.) And I'm here to share what I have learned with other women so that they can use my story to feel seen, heard, and validated. I'm here to share what I have learned so that others can learn, too.

So what have I learned?

The awareness, and the self compassion, and the acceptance don't make the difficult things go away – but it sure gives them less power. The weaker they get, the stronger I get. The more that I learn, love, and accept the flawed and hard parts of myself, the quieter those voices in my head get that try stirring up the fear.

Rising is never finished, because falling is never finished. There will always be bumps along the way, so how many times can you pick yourself back up when things are hard? It's okay to have days where you barely make it off the couch. It's okay to have days where you feel like you can do all the things (these days usually come before the days that land you on the couch). It's all okay. You're not lazy or failing or less valuable. It's the self-love, self-awareness and self-compassion that gets you through. It's the grace you give yourself that replaces the shame that gets you through. It's the boundaries and the authenticity to your true self that gets you through. It's meeting your needs without guilt and justification that gets you through.

It's your investment of your own love and making yourself a priority that gets you through. Things are still going to be hard, but as Glennon Doyle told us all – we can do hard things[1].

After going through – and continuing to go through – all of the things that I do, I wouldn't be able to make it through the inevitable hard days without the compassion I have for me. You deserve it, too.

To the women here reading my story right now: I want you to know that everything that makes you, you – is beautiful. There is nothing "wrong" with you. The unique individual you are is so important, and learning more and more about her is equally as important. The more you learn and the more you advocate for yourself, the more stock and energy you put into meeting your needs and being authentic, the more you create a safe place inside yourself for love, care, and compassion, the more you will feel your innate value as a woman. There is no greater power for creating strength than valuing yourself and regarding yourself as highly as you regard the other people in your life that you love.

If you take one thing away from this chapter, I hope that it is that you need to be seen for who you REALLY are. The hiding, pretending, and putting yourself last will only bring you to burnout (or worse), and you will inevitably need to bring the authentic woman inside of you out and give her what she needs in order to heal. You deserve love and compassion in all forms from all of the humans in your life that are close to you, and you deserve it now exactly as you are. The most IMPORTANT person to receive that love, compassion, and validation

---

1 Doyle, G. (2020). *Untamed.* Dial Press.

from – is yourself. There is only one you. You are unique and special, and no one can be you like you can.

My story will continue after this chapter, and so will yours. So please, do me a favour and make your story, YOUR story. You are the author of your best life and you are the creator of your "woman rising." The voice inside you telling you what you need and what you desire is there. Maybe it's through physical feelings you get, or in actual whispers. She may be a bit buried, but she's there, and she's telling you something.

Listen to her.

RISING IS NEVER FINISHED, BECAUSE FALLING IS NEVER FINISHED.

DANIELLE CHAPUT

AUTHOR PHOTO: ABBI LONGO | LA VIE PHOTOGRAPHY
INSTAGRAM: @DEE.TAPPINGINTOWELLNESS
TAPPINGINTOWELLNESS.CA

CHAPTER 5

I've always been a person who is comfortable in the hospital. That's weird I know; it's not the most favourite of places for a lot of people, but it was for me. It was a place where I felt confident and I felt empowered. It was a place where I knew implicitly what I was supposed to do and why I was there.

I've been a Registered Nurse for 14 years, and I can't remember a time in my life when this wasn't what I wanted to do. I was that five-year-old with the nurse's costume and kit at Christmas – NOT the doctor – the nurse.

I remember the first day that I knew I wanted to be a nurse like it was yesterday. I was eight years old and we had just gone on a field trip to the hospital (which seems insane now, but we did). We went on a tour of the hospital and we went to the NICU. I got to see all the little babies in their incubators and I absolutely fell in love with the thought of being that nurse in scrubs working there. That was my first glimpse into nursing and that desire never left me. I can see that day so clearly in my mind, right down to the jeans I was wearing and the turquoise top I had on.

And just as clearly, I can remember the day in 2020 when my faith was shaken and I didn't know if I could be a nurse anymore. That was the day that led to a breakdown. The breakdown that forever changed me, altered my path, and led me down a road that I never expected to go.

You see, being a nurse is not only a profession, not just a job you do to pay the bills. It becomes a core part of your identity. And at that time, I lost who I was. Henry David Thoreau said, "It is not until we are lost, do we begin to find ourselves."[2] It's a saying that I have subscribed to over these last couple of years. It stuck out to me and gave me hope and a reminder that I was finding myself through this. That breakdown and loss of identity had to happen, for me to discover who I truly am and what I have to offer in this world.

My name is Danielle. I'm a Registered Nurse of 14 years who works in the Intensive Care Unit, and I am an EFT (Emotional Freedom Technique) practitioner. I am a wife and mom to three busy boys. I have struggled the last few years with Generalized Anxiety Disorder, burnout, compassion fatigue and vicarious trauma.

There are three specific aspects to this story that I think shape this path for me: early motherhood, the crumbling of my nursing identity, and finding the emotional freedom technique, and I am going to lay it all bare with you here. This is my story of how I went from losing myself in nursing and motherhood – to discovering my voice and becoming an entrepreneur and by founding my company, Tapping Into Wellness. I found my mother f*ing passion for living life wholeheartedly and in authenticity! I discovered my way to a place that I didn't expect, and I can't wait to share my story with you; so let's get to it!

---

2 Goodreads. (n.d.). *Henry David Thoreau* . Goodreads. Retrieved September 13, 2022, from https://www.goodreads.com/quotes/28969-not-till-we-are-lost-in-other-words-not-till

Let's rewind here, and go back in time a little bit to the beginning of my story in 2019. I was a new mom to three boys (3 kids under 3 years old, holy hell what were we thinking?!). I likely had a bit of postpartum anxiety that went undiagnosed at that time. Three pregnancies in four years had taken a toll on both my mental and physical health.

While I love being a mom to all of these boys, I found that I had lost who I was outside of mothering. I attached my value and worth to how good of a mom I was. This is BAD news. As anyone with kids can tell you, no matter how good of a parent you are, you will have good and bad days with those little beings.

I had many run-ins with good old anxiety, one of the worst coming about a month after our third son was born. My husband went back to work after some paternity leave time, and it was my first night alone with all three boys. My husband is a nurse and was on shift. One of my biggest fears at the time was that all three boys would wake up at once, and I wouldn't be able to settle them all. I was literally petrified of this occurrence. Lo and behold, what do you think happened that first night? The baby was up nursing, the toddler (12 months old… barely a toddler) was up screaming and wanted me and only me to himself. By some grace of God, the three-year-old stayed asleep, but it didn't matter. I was spinning, and my spinning was making them spin. I remember calling my Mum to come over at midnight, and I called my husband on his break bawling.

Luckily, my husband was able to scoot home (hello superhero!) and my mum flew over to help. I had never felt like such a failure in all of my life. Such a seemingly small thing, which seems like no big deal when I look at it now, had derailed me. It was one of my lowest points as a mom, BECAUSE I had attached my own self-worth to a situation that I couldn't possibly have total control over. I made it mean something about me. There was a problem – but I was too deep in it to see it and continued to push through. I figured this was motherhood in the trenches with little ones and that I was supposed to feel this way.

Those first few years of my youngest son's life were all about survival mode. Making it through the day with coffee after coffee, and falling into bed. I was putting myself dead last and ignoring the signs that my body was giving me. I was really struggling with my worth, keeping up appearances, and being able to do all the things.

Somewhere along the line, an ad for a fitness program came up and it was then that I joined a local fitness company (shout out to Keepfit Women and Jeenie!), and decided to give myself some dedicated "me time" outside of the house. I got a taste of what making myself a priority felt like, and a glimmer of how much better of a mom I became when I took care of myself first.

This program not only helped me to get my body moving, but it also taught me a lot about self-confidence and self-worth, and I began to see myself in a different light. I was fortunate enough to have a fire lit inside of me from that experience. That's really what kick-started my transition into valuing myself and prioritizing my needs and desires – which I am ever-so-grateful for.

I was carrying on nicely down this path to self-discovery and doing all the right things to look after myself properly when – BOOM! 2020 hit and that's when the path got a little bit crazy and things changed in a way that I didn't see coming.

I remember coming into work in April of 2020, and caring for a gentleman in his sixties. He wasn't doing well, and he wasn't going to survive. I remember going to my physician colleague to ask for support and I was told "he's dying; what do you want me to do?"

You see, that gentleman was one of many dying that day. One of many that needed our undivided attention and couldn't have it. The physician left to tend to another emergency situation and I remember feeling so alone and scared. This was at the start of the pandemic and because of the nature of our healthcare environment at the time, visitors were not allowed to come into the hospital. Families couldn't be present with their loved ones so a lot of people died alone. A lot of people died with us by their sides in lieu of their family.

Once we had all the logistics finalized and we knew that we weren't going to be performing any heroic measures on this gentleman, I called his family and expressed that to them. I was able to secure special permission for his family to come in, but they decided that they weren't able to be by his side for those final moments. This is not an uncommon thing.

Holding hands with death is not something that a lot of people can do, but it's something that I take extreme pride in in my work.

I am grateful that I was able to give them a form of peace at that moment, but it was far from peaceful for me. I remember sitting in his room telling him stories that his brother had shared with me about their long-standing rivalry between the Montreal Canadiens and the Toronto Maple Leafs. I remember teasing him the way that his brother would have, holding his hand and telling him that his brother can't be here today, so I am his brother's hands and that he wasn't alone. His brother had told me his favourite music and I sat with him and I held his hand and I sang, in probably the most unattractive, off-key voice. All of this with hopes of bringing him some comfort.

At this time in the hospital, we were fully isolated. We had baby monitors in the patient rooms where we could communicate with our colleagues without having to open the doors or remove our equipment. I remember sitting with this gentleman in all of my gear, my visor half fogged up and looking through the window behind me. I saw three of my colleagues standing there crying at the window, having heard me speaking to my patient through the monitor. I could see in their eyes that they knew how I was feeling. I remember staying with him until his final breath and then I called his brother to let him know.

I remember my colleagues breaking down around me, but to me, it was just another day at work. (Except that it wasn't.) Something broke in me that day. A task that I have done so many times before – being there for the death of a person, being that "go-to," that rock, that individual who guides a family through that loss – felt hollow. It was sad, of course, but it also felt empty. I felt scared and uncomfortable, like this may not be the thing that I can continue doing anymore.

During Covid, there was a lot of death. It became necessary to become somewhat numb to it. There were a lot of those days and a lot of times when families weren't allowed to be present in the hospital to be with their loved ones. As nurses, we would sit with these families on video chat, and act as an extension of them. Supporting their loved ones and trying to support them virtually through a screen.

In that loss of human connection, I lost my connection to nursing. I lost my ability to find dignity in what we did and in my confidence as a practitioner to provide comfort. All of the sudden, our world had been turned upside down and I didn't know how to do my job in this environment.

That was the day that I fell out of love with nursing and started to feel disconnected. Looking back now, I think that this loss of identity was one of the best things that could have happened to me, but at the moment, it was devastating, terrifying, and confusing.

Being a nurse is still a huge part of who I am today. I don't believe that I will ever be able to let that part of me go, but it no longer defines me. I have been working with my therapist to become at peace with this change and to work through a sort of grieving process for myself. It felt like I had lost all of myself right along with the profession that I so loved, and much like I did with mothering, I had attached a lot of my own self-image and self-worth to being a nurse.

When we are so tied to our titles and the stories that we tell ourselves about who we are, we limit our capacity for what we think we can reach and the person that we could potentially be, if we were to let go of those things.

If I hadn't let go of feeling to my core that what I am is a nurse, I never would have gone down the untraditional path that I ended up going down to create Tapping Into Wellness. Being Western medicine trained, looking to Eastern medicine and holistic modalities isn't typical. So if I hadn't let go of that identity of myself, if I hadn't been forced to see past that, I would have missed out on experiencing a whole side of myself that I didn't even know existed.

During the pandemic, my husband was also a front-line ICU nurse. This doubled our exposure, doubled our worries, and added to our anxieties around what we were bringing home to our children. While my husband was working, I was home, and while I was working, he was home. Coupling this with the fact that we were homeschooling our three children (a teacher, a nurse does not make, trust me lol), we were faced with more than our fair share of challenges and stressors.

The day this came to a head for me, my husband was at work and I was sitting in our laundry room with a pile of dirty clothes beneath me, folding what felt like the hundredth load of laundry for the day. In the background, my kids were on their virtual class calls and we had been stuck in the house for three days. The world was on lockdown and their competing school schedules left no time during the day to get out for fresh air or do anything other than their school work. I could feel the walls closing in around me. I could feel the tightness in my chest, the heaviness in my head, and the tears welling behind my eyes. I was stressed out and overwhelmed. I knew something had to change.

I found myself listening to a podcast about improving your sleep because I hadn't been sleeping well (gee, I wonder why?!). On the podcast, the person they were interviewing was talking about tapping a.k.a. EFT. During the interview, she led the listeners of the podcast through a five-minute tapping session around decreasing stress, overwhelm, and anxiety. Sitting amidst the dirty laundry with tears streaming down my face, I thought, *what the hell do I have to lose?*

Being a Western medicine-trained ICU nurse, I felt that I was above these holistic practices. They always felt a little "woo-woo" to me, if I'm being honest, but I had reached a breaking point and nothing else had helped. So I listened to her guided session and I tapped, and I breathed, and I repeated back to her the statements that she was saying.

While I did so, I felt such a powerful calm and shift in my energy happen – that I was dumbfounded. What the heck just happened? There is no possible way that tapping points on my body made me feel this much better. While a big part of me still doubted the effectiveness of the tapping, something inside of me felt compelled to follow through with it – to create this as a practice for myself and to see if this good feeling could continue.

I started using tapping as a personal practice. I integrated it slowly into my day, tapping before bed or in the morning, tapping a few points here and there when I was feeling anxious or overwhelmed and frustrated. And as I did so, I felt things inside of me start to shift and change. I became more open to acknowledging my anxiety and releasing the stigmas that I felt around that.

Despite being a nurse knowing better about stigmas and knowing better about the importance of mental health, I felt like a failure. I felt lost and confused, alone and embarrassed. I decided to use tapping as a way to work through these emotions. I started acknowledging the truth of how I was feeling, instead of trying to push it aside and carry on.

Facing my feelings and emotions with a practice that worked for me knocked down barriers. I found myself reaching out to a psychotherapist and starting therapy sessions. I reached out to my doctor for support with my generalized anxiety disorder and started seeking treatment options. My doctor had previously suggested medication to me when my children were younger, but I refused it at the time, not wanting to acknowledge the fact that there was an issue.

There was a problem with the way that I was coping in my environment, and when I tapped and released those emotions, I felt empowered. I felt like I didn't need to hide anymore. I was able to embrace my differences as the superpowers that they are. I felt in control of the situation and knew that my anxiety did not define me, but that it was, in fact, just a part of me.

I started therapy and medication, and I continued my tapping practice to heal myself. For me, the medication was a starting point, a way to clear the fog and step into my true power, authenticity, and transparency.

There is still so much stigma around mental health and reaching out for help and I want to change that by sharing this with others. I want to give those around me the same tools and support that I have been given in order to provide them with a feeling of empowerment and the ability to grow and to live authentically in their wholehearted life without embarrassment, without feeling the stigma or the need to hide what they were going through.

Tapping became such a valuable tool for me in so many ways that I knew that I had to bring this underutilized practice to the surface. I knew in my gut that this is what came next for me, and that I was meant to carve out this path. I was meant to share my experiences, and in doing so, I would enable someone else to possibly try something for themselves that they hadn't considered before. Thus, Tapping Into Wellness was born.

Creating Tapping Into Wellness seems like a dream sometimes and I catch myself wondering if I'm actually doing it. Can I actually call myself a business owner and CEO? It feels surreal and exciting and terrifying all at once. It's hard not to get caught up in the imposter syndrome and to not be discouraged when things don't go according to plan.

I've certainly experienced my ups and downs on this journey so far, but I've come to realize that all I can really do is act on my gut reactions – do what feels good to me, and what is meant for me will be, so I can't possibly screw it up. I'm loving this journey that I'm on and I am grateful every day that I took a chance on something different.

The darkest moments of my career as a nurse shone a light on something that I never expected. If you were to ask me five years ago if this is what I saw for my future, I would have probably laughed in your face and scoffed something along the lines of, "No, I'm a nurse; that's who I am." And while I am still a nurse, I know that it is not my only truth. I know unequivocally that I am supposed to be on this path that I found by accident. Helping other people find their power, happiness, fulfilment, and peace lights me up like nothing I have ever done before.

The nursing world continues to crumble around me, and that's a hard reality to deal with. This career that I have built, invested in, and loved – has changed. That is incredibly sad to see. I don't know if that part will ever get easier, but I do know that whatever happens, I will be okay. I am not defined by my role there. My identity is not nursing. My identity lies in helping and empowering others to live authentically and wholeheartedly.

Life ebbs and flows. Life gives you challenges to overcome and barriers to work around. But when we open our eyes to looking for opportunities in places that we never thought to look before, we learn about ourselves. We discover our purpose and we see all of the signals that we've been bypassing with our tunnel vision in the past. Imagine the potential that's just sitting there waiting for you on the other side of the titles; on the other side of the stories that we tell ourselves about who we are, what we are capable of, and what defines us. These are part of our limiting beliefs, and these are now a part of what I help others overcome with EFT.

If you are struggling right now – maybe you're facing a mental health challenge like I was, or maybe your entire identity has been uprooted like mine was, and you feel lost – I want you to know that there is light on the other side of that darkness. There is discomfort in growth. I believe that I was too comfortable in nursing. Discomfort had to be created for me to be shaken up enough to look for other opportunities that would allow me to find my true path, my next step, and my purpose.

So when those discomforts come for you, I encourage you to lean into them. Look beyond them and be open to the experiences that you may not have expected. I hope that in reading this chapter, you have come to see how much opportunity there is out there for you, no matter where you are in your journey.

And if you are reading this and you happen to be a nurse or healthcare provider who's working in a similar environment as me, I hope you gained a little solace in knowing that you are not alone in your feelings and that there is more beyond what you're seeing right now.

So if there's one message that I want to leave you with, it's to trust in yourself and to trust the process. Know that the night truly is always darkest before the dawn, and that those moments where it all comes crashing down are making room for something amazing.

It will be okay.
You can do this.

DANIELLE PENDLETON

INSTAGRAM: @LUMOSMORTGAGES
FACEBOOK: @DANIELLEPENDLETON
LINKEDIN @DANIELLEPENDLETON

CHAPTER 6

I'm Danielle Pendleton.

I'm a not-so-closet nerd who's a sucker for problem-solving, spreadsheets, Marvel, Harry Potter, Lord of the Rings references, and delicious food. I love long walks on the beach (cliché, I know, but it's true). Travelling the world and learning new languages feeds my soul and I somehow manage to pair dill pickles with almost anything while treating chips as an extra food group despite my foodie and fine dining tendencies. My 90lb beast of a pup Lleial and rescue kitty Skittles remind me that you can find joy in the most unexpected things, and I thrive on challenges because I see them as growth opportunities. I'm still getting accustomed to the whole "You are responsible for your emotions and reactions, but you are NOT responsible for those of others" concept, especially when it comes to potentially hurt feelings and seeing anyone suffer. I'm a lover, not a fighter. I'm going to talk a lot about my own experiences here because that's how I relate to people, and try to show that I feel compassion and care for them. I'll start with my stories, and go into how I overcame and rose above all of the chaos, bullshit, devastation, hurt, trauma, and my Neurodivergency.

I was bullied for most of my life: in childhood, through school, in the serving/bar industry, and even in my current industry that I've been in for years. I was labelled as "too energetic, annoying, and too nice." I believed what, who, and how others told me I needed to be for a long time. I thought that I could "fix" people and that I was just overly sensitive. I shrunk in the classroom, the workplace, and away from my peers while simultaneously acting out for attention, desperate to be liked. And you know where it got me? It almost killed me, multiple times. I used to hide the fact that to this day, I'm still shocked that I graduated from the University of Alberta with a Bachelor of Commerce Degree because of how much I struggled. I never had the opportunity to explore and understand my neurodiversity (let alone things like my sexuality) in my teens because I attended fully Francophone Catholic schools that were pretty cliquey and judgmental. I definitely didn't fit in no matter how I tried. In my early 20s, I wound up in an all-around abusive relationship with someone who had a history of dating younger women who often hadn't yet found themselves, leaving them more vulnerable to his narcissistic abuse and gaslighting. The emotional and psychological abuse was worse than the physical, because at least physical abuse left marks and made the thought of leaving easier rather than me being labelled as "overly sensitive."

You wouldn't believe what changed the perspective in my brain so that I felt strong enough, sure enough, and safe enough to finally leave that toxic relationship: jumping out of a plane 10,000 ft. above an island and the open ocean. Something clicked during the free-fall, and I thought you're going to be okay, you can do this. In that moment I realized how powerful our mind and thoughts could be. The next time I was verbally and emotionally attacked, I grabbed my stuff and left, finally sharing the situation with my parents so that I knew I couldn't go back, regardless of the things that he said and tried. To this day, I regret not filing a formal police report so that others could be warned about him, but I was still afraid to enrage him, many years later. Now?

Fuck being afraid. Fuck being silenced. Fuck falling in line. And fuck bullies.

I AM thankful for the people that I've been fortunate to surround myself with at a point in time or most of my life. I'm thankful for my boyfriend, my mom and dad, my friends – both new and old, and for those that stayed with me and loved me for who I am. To the one who let me crash "girls night" the night I left; to the one who outright said "I don't like how he speaks to you" after that dinner; to the one who lovingly reminded me that I was being severely gaslit despite their connection to that now ex; and to the ones who have supported me and reminded me that my mental health and myself come first: you all changed my life for the better. Thank you. I still sometimes expect "the other shoe to drop," as they say, but it doesn't – not by chance, but by the fruit of my efforts in surrounding myself with incredible humans.

I try to lend my voice or platforms whenever and however I can. I'm very open and passionate about mental health and Neurodivergency, especially when it comes to shedding light and helping fellow Neurodivergents feel even a little more seen or understood when it comes to ADHD. If I can help a single person who is struggling, being vulnerable is completely worth it to me. That fills my cup. As someone who doesn't want progeny of her own, this is meant to be a bit of a legacy to me. This is the way I feel that I can help make a difference. If we all encompassed empathy while trying to make a positive difference in this world, and if we all worked to be the positive change that we want to see in the world, don't you agree that this world would be so much better?

I have ADHD. What does that even mean? I actually don't have an Attention Hyperactivity Deficit "disorder" though, do I? It's truly more of an "Executive Dysfunction and Hormonal/Emotional Dysregulation Disorder" because not only does my brain not produce enough Dopamine naturally, it doesn't regulate several other things as much as it needs to, so I'm always fighting myself in addition the outside world. There are so many myths about ADHD that tend to cloud one's understanding of it, and if I don't understand myself, how can others? People with ADHD aren't just "hyper", "stupid," or "lazy." Labels and stigmas like these are hurtful, untrue, and can stay with us for our lifetimes, deeply scarring us, among other things. Furthermore, they make light of the ways that we are disabled.

Have you ever had to try to explain to someone that you couldn't finish or do something because your brain literally wouldn't let you? If you haven't or don't get how this is possible, please pay attention: If one's Executive Function is fucked, the struggle is fucking REAL.

Have you heard of Sensory Processing Disorder? I hadn't until last year (2021) when I was rendered completely useless, unable to read, process, or understand any of the written content at the "Beyond Van Gogh Exhibit" where I live. My brain was literally panicking. I didn't understand what was happening so I could barely speak and communicate to my cousin and to my boyfriend, let alone explain what they were witnessing - which was me crumbling, bawling, being extremely slow at each station, and trying to keep it together while not understanding what on earth was happening other than feeling broken.

Fun fact: Neurotypicals cannot only have completely silent or quiet brains, without any narrative, but also their brains automatically know how to filter out the right sounds…Yep, some lucky peoples' brains basically have built-in noise-cancelling "brain-buds."

Learning this blew my mind last year, but also saved my ears as I started carrying around (and eventually invested in) a decent pair of earplugs without shame. Who knew that, all this time, my brain just didn't know how to filter out the background and foreground noises? It literally was missing the filter and instead hears all voices and noises at the same booming sound level. I grieved those opportunities when people thought I was being rude, weird, or even stupid, in which things could've been different had I known.

Have you ever been told what you "are" by someone else? How about by almost everyone else, and maybe at some point you've given up thinking anything about yourself because you don't see the point? Instead, you may have had trouble at not only knowing, but trusting in who you are, or even trusting in what you truly know? If not, I'm happy for you!

But if so, I'm here to tell you that I've more than been there: I've lived it and sometimes still feel like I'm coming out on the other side. I want to gently remind you that you deserve better than that and to be kind to yourself. I'm here to say as someone who is Neurodivergent (ND) that you might spend your entire life being told that you're things you're not - and if so, it IS total bullshit. These are myths, and I'm here to try and help break them, because fuck them and the pain that they create.

Myth #1 Everyone with ADHD "is Hyper(-active)"

Myth #2 We're Stupid

Myth #3 We're Lazy and Need to Try Harder

Of those without the fortune of being Neurotypical (NT) - whose brains function as they should - not one person WISHES that they were Neurodivergent. They may wish to be seen and to be recognized and understood as such, but no one actually *hopes* to have to deal with any of the above or what really comes with it. It honestly simultaneously hurts and pisses me off when what can truly disable me becomes the butt of countless jokes, and when I'm treated as if I chose my Neurodivergencies, let alone have to fight tooth-and-nail for the solutions that have helped me try to successfully navigate an unforgiving Neurotypical-expectant world. We are often treated as though we chose for society to generally reject us and to tell us we aren't being good enough or trying enough, and to be treated like an inconvenience or a burden. Like we chose to automatically be contrarian, to have horrible short-term memories and fight what Cady Herring would call "word vomit," never fitting in and constantly fighting both ourselves and our Executive Dysfunction. I'm here to lovingly remind you that whatever NDs you have or Spectrum(s) that you may find yourself on, those who matter don't mind, and those who mind don't matter.

I'm considered one of the "lucky" ones, because as a kid, I physically exhibited so many "hyperactivity and inattentive" symptoms that I was formally diagnosed with ADHD. In contrast, most women don't actually get diagnosed and understand themselves until their 30s-50s. I am 30 years old now, and in the last year, I've learned more about myself and my "issues" than in the first twenty-something years of my life. I've mourned a bit. I've mourned the opportunities that I could've had if I, my loved ones, friends, bosses, coworkers, co-students, and society as a whole understood what having ADHD actually meant for me.

I've already managed to go off on many classic ADHD tangents, so I'm going to come to my original question: Have you ever been told what you are…by someone else? How about by almost everyone else, and maybe at some point, you've given up thinking, anything about yourself because you don't see the point? There IS a point - in fact, there are countless reasons - so please remember that our brains can be SO much louder and harder on ourselves than we should be! Many of us get by in an NT-expected-society thanks to several things that tend to hurt us harder, immediately, or further down the road: we can act out, shrink, or mask.

How did I get through it? Well, to be completely honest, I'm still a work-in-progress, and as a lifelong seeker of knowledge and improvement, I always will be. My people were a massive help, my resilience and learning/continuing to work on prioritizing and forgiving myself. As a way of masking, many of us strive to be perfectionists, overly helpful, etc. I've been learning so much about myself and my neurodiversity, which has been critical. Understanding why my brain and body react the way they do has helped me and those around me so much.

I've been called some of the following so many times by not only my peers and superiors, but by those I held close to me and trusted. I was labelled, made fun of, excluded, and ostracized from the time I was a kid to a teen and even into early adulthood. I rarely stuck up for myself because I believed them. Unfortunately, I trusted that I was these things because these labels and assumptions were rigorously thrust onto me:

- *Lazy*
- *Annoying*
- *Loud*
- *Bossy*
- *A Nerd/Geek (as if it was a bad thing)*
- *Anal/Overly Particular about things*

- *"Too much"*
- *Heterosexual*
- *A Try-Hard*
- *A Tease (because I wouldn't "put out" when men felt they deserved sexual acts from me)*
- *Broken*
- *Not Enough*

Trauma doesn't automatically result in growth or strength. It can make one more sensitive or shut down from one's feelings, extremely hyper-vigilant, wary, dependent on others or hyper-independent, and prone to avoidance. Once I started to truly dig and learn about how my brain functions, and why it and my body does what it does, everything changed:

- *I learned that I sometimes would eat or shop as methods to seek stimulation and dopamine, rather than because I simply needed to.*
- *I experience enormous validation in knowing that I am not alone when it comes to having "safe foods" and foods/meals that I can eat on repeat and then suddenly not touch for months afterwards, and that it is literally possible to forget or not be able to eat certain things due to dysregulation…*
- *Music has always been an escape for me, but it needs to hit "just right" for me to feel either relaxed, motivated, stimulated, or to derive dopamine from it.*
- *As someone who is quite tactile, I invested in a memory foam "bean bag" chair and I often pair it with my weighted blanket for DE-stimulation and to reset, rest, relax, reprieve, and rejuvenate. As a chronic insomniac, sometimes these are the only ways I can get some sleep.*
- *Therapy is severely underrated and stigmatized, but everyone should go. My therapist is amazing and I'm so thankful for him.*
- *I began trying to educate those around me in hopes that they could understand me better and accept me more, and so that there would be understanding as to why I do and am the way that I am.*

- *This really helped me learn who my real friends were, and who loved me as I am – which really helped with my RSD and insecurities.*
- *I will never forget when a friend of mine said to me "I admire that you aren't afraid to ask for what you want" – it made me tear up and my heart swell with love and warmth. It was the day after a family member had shamed me for doing just that, calling me "selfish" when I had meant no malintent of the sort. I'm a "you don't know if you don't try" type of person, and some would be shocked to learn where that's gotten me at times. It's all about perspective!*

These things have been critical for my recovery from severe burnout and trauma from multiple car accidents, concussions, and from trusting and/or doing too much. I'm actually still concussed while I put this together so it's been fun!

Have you realized it yet? The fact that our society and world tends to reject those that don't follow the norm, regardless of whether it's of their own volition or not (such as NDs). What if a perspective-shift would change everything? Think about it: if Neurotypicals don't have to fight to achieve what can take my entire day's energy and will to accomplish, it seems like some things need to change.

I am Danielle Pendleton: an optimist, a bleeding heart, a problem-solver, a feminist, a partner, a friend, a daughter, a woman…I am adaptable, kind, and caring – sometimes it hurts and that's okay. I am stellar at what I do, and I am loving. I am determined, I am powerful, and I am strong as hell. My Executive Dysfunction is a part of me, but I am not my Executive Dysfunction. I have picked myself up more times than not, and I've come so far - much farther than I ever thought I would. I have so much to be proud of, which I am beyond thankful for. And so do you. You've got this.

JANET RENNIE

INSTAGRAM: @JANET.RENNIE.16

CHAPTER 7

I remember the first time that postpartum depression was brought up in conversation. I was about seven months along with my twins, and my sister-in-law had warned my husband to watch out for it once I gave birth. I had heard about it, thought that I knew the basics of what was involved, and agreed that my husband should watch for it. Did I really think it would affect me? I didn't think so; I was overjoyed to be a soon-to-be mama. I laugh now at how naive I was. I had no idea what was coming for me.

My children weren't even 24 hours old when postpartum anxiety hit me like a freight train. I can't even tell you when the depression hit, because I honestly don't remember. I was so lost in a fog that I, sadly, barely remember the first few months of my kiddos' lives.

My name is Janet. I'm a stay-at-home mama to my twin toddlers, a wife, an author, and an amateur photographer. This is the story of my battle with postpartum anxiety and depression.

My labor and delivery were difficult. My daughter did not want to come out, (stubborn like both of her parents) and needed assistance. My son came two minutes later, and I still remember the shout from the doctor, "CODE PINK!" Something was hit on the wall, and all of a sudden, "code pink" was being called over the intercom as the door to the OR opened and 10 staff members rushed in, surrounding my son.

I was terrified. I couldn't see him, hadn't heard him cry, and had no idea what code pink stood for. One of my delivery nurses came over and told me that my son wasn't breathing. I immediately started to cry, and turned to my husband demanding that he follow my son if they took him from the room. It probably wasn't even two minutes later that he began to cry. Even though the nurse told me that he was okay and was breathing properly now, I could not stop the tears from flowing.

That night, even though my babies were sleeping, and so was my husband, I couldn't. I sat on the edge of the bed, staring at both of the bassinets, watching their tiny tummies rise and fall, even standing up and gently laying my hand on them to make sure they were rising. I couldn't help but think that my son not breathing, and my daughter being stuck, was my fault. I should've just opted for a c-section like my doctor had suggested when we found out I was having twins. This is when my anxiety began to take over my brain, any rational thoughts began to disappear, leaving only the worst case scenario, and what the hell had you done to your children.

We stayed in the hospital for four days. During that time, I barely slept, and I barely ate. I was surviving on tea from the coffee shop downstairs, and an occasional bagel if I was able to stomach it. I felt like if I fell asleep for even a second, my babies would need me and I wouldn't hear them. Looking back, that probably wouldn't have happened considering they slept maybe a foot from my bed. I felt sick. I worried constantly. Why couldn't I get them to stop crying? Were they eating enough? Why were they losing weight, and now they were down from their birth weight? When they were sleeping, I spent my time googling. Please, do NOT do that, seriously, Google is not your friend.

Before we finally got to leave, a woman came in, someone who arranged visits at home to ensure that you and your child(ren) are settling in. I didn't see it as being helpful. What I saw was someone who already had me pinpointed as a mother who was going to lose her shit, and hurt her children. I politely answered her questions, listened to her speech, and then adamantly refused to allow home visits. After she left the room, I lost it on my husband, who I was convinced had gone behind my back to the nurses and stated that I was already having difficulty and would need to be checked on. This, of course, wasn't the case, but you try telling that to an anxiety-ridden mother who's been running on maybe ten hours of sleep since she gave birth four days ago. This would be the first of many battles that my husband and I would have while I was trying to survive in my own personal hell.

Our first night home, my anxiety spiked again when it was time to put the babies down for bed. I had seen no issue while pregnant, about the twins sleeping in their own room, as it was literally right across the hall from our room. When the time came to put them in their cribs, I panicked. After four days of having them literally within arm's reach of me, there was no way that I could stand having them in their own room. What if they stopped breathing? This resulted in me trying to put the playpen together with the bassinet insert so that they could stay in the room with my husband and me.

Well, unbeknownst to us, and my parents who had purchased the playpen for us, it had been sold broken. Cut to me, having a breakdown on the floor of my bedroom at 11:00 p.m. when I could not put this playpen together. Finally, the babies did indeed go to sleep in their crib; yes crib, we put the two of them in the same crib. Then my husband fell asleep in the rocking chair, and I fell asleep on the floor of their nursery. This was my preference, as stitches were not conducive to sitting down comfortably for any length of time.

Fast-forward to three weeks later.

My husband had two weeks off, then he had to go back to work. We were at the point in Covid where we were no longer on a work-from-home lockdown. Luckily for me, my mother and mother-in-law, were trading off days where they would come and stay all day, helping me.

I was having difficulty adjusting. I still wasn't really eating or sleeping, and couldn't remember the last time that I had worn something other than pajamas or washed my hair. What was the point? I had nowhere to go, and no one besides my mother/mother in law who saw me. It's not like my newborns could tell that Mommy was in the same outfit as yesterday.

I didn't realize that not even wanting to get dressed because it was too much effort was a symptom of the depression that had already taken hold of me. There were days when I handed a baby off to whichever mother was there because I couldn't stand the thought of holding them for one more second. When I couldn't get them to stop crying, or to go to sleep, and the grandmothers could, I wondered what the hell was wrong with me. What was it about me or what was I not doing? I was their mother. How could I not figure this out?

I started to resent my choice to have children. I resented the fact that I had had twins. I was a first-time mom! Why couldn't I just have one child to learn how to be a mom? I thought I had been prepared for what having twins was going to be, but honestly, until you're there in the trenches, you have no idea what you are in for.

I thought for sure that I had ruined our lives by having children – and told my husband so. He told me that I needed to speak to my doctor, because there was something wrong. I ignored him. *Oh, he just thinks I'm crazy.* I reached out to my sister-in-law with my struggles, and she listened without judgment, which I am so thankful for. She encouraged me to see my doctor, and she assured me that the solution was not to take my kids away. It's because of her encouragement that I eventually reached out, even though I was terrified.

After a consult with my doctor, she put me on medication that she said would help bring me back into balance. While this helped a little, it didn't stop the mood swings, rage, and depression spirals.

I began to have very dark thoughts; thoughts that I didn't share with anyone else, because I didn't want to admit what was going on in my head. Everyone else had such an easier time with my children than I did, so what was the point of me still being around? My babies were only a month old, it's not like they would miss me (at least that's what I was telling myself). They would be better off if they didn't have to deal with their mother crying when they cried, or yelling (yes yelling at my brand new babes) when I couldn't figure out what they wanted or how to make them stop crying.

A friend told me when they were about a week old, to enjoy this time because it was the "honeymoon" stage. I didn't understand what she meant by that. Honeymoon stage? What about having babies that cried all of the time was a honeymoon? Looking back, I realize that she meant that they eat, sleep, poop – and that's pretty much it. You can cart them wherever the heck you want (except not during Covid; I didn't have that opportunity). I resented that my husband got to leave the house alone for several hours a day, get a break from them, not have to listen to crying, and speak to adults.

On the rare occasion that I did leave the house with my kids, it was usually to walk them. Even this small thing caused me severe anxiety. I began to panic about what I would do if they started to fuss or cry while I was out walking them. Would people immediately start staring and commenting about why I couldn't soothe my own children? *Oh, she's a bad mom. Look, she can't even calm her kids down.* When I was out with them, I would get stopped and passerbys would gush. "Oh look how cute they are! Oh twins?! Million dollar family, oh what blessings they are, you're so lucky!" I just smiled and nodded, when all I wanted to do is shout at the top of my lungs, *Do you know how fucking hard this is?! I don't know what I'm doing! I'm drowning here! This is awful!* But you can't say that. At least I felt like I couldn't. I had tried very hard for a long time to have my kids, and now here they were. How dare I say that it was difficult? That I was struggling? That sometimes I second-guessed my decision? I was having a major case of the "you shoulds." You *should* be grateful. You *should* be enjoying every second. You *should* be happy all the time. This is far from how I felt, and I felt (still feel) a ton of guilt that I don't enjoy every second that I am with my kids.

I remember in the early days, I was having a conversation in my kitchen about how much I was struggling, and how I wondered why this was all so hard. The reply I received is that you wanted babies, this is what having babies is. That has stuck with me, through all of my struggles. See, I believed it when it was said to me, and that was wrong. Having babies doesn't mean that you have to be happy all the time. Having babies doesn't mean that it's not gonna be hard as hell. Having babies doesn't mean that you have to enjoy every second or you're not a good mom. I let that fester in my mind and it made me miserable. It was not what I needed to hear.

If I could go back, I would say that what I really needed is for someone to listen to me. I didn't need to be fixed or criticized. I just needed to be allowed to say everything that was on my mind without being judged for it.

Trust Your Instincts

Even before my children were born, I was overwhelmed by other people's opinions about my mothering. *Are you breastfeeding or bottle feeding? Breast is best you know, they won't bond if you bottle feed! Are you staying home or going back to work? Staying home, really? I guess your husband doesn't mind supporting you.*

Once my twins were born, these opinions became a hundred-fold from family, friends, and even strangers on the street. I constantly felt like my instincts weren't good enough, that the way I was choosing to raise my children was wrong. Any decision that I made about them, I agonized over. It kept me up at night. What would our families think if I chose to do something that wasn't what they suggested? I would receive opinions that I didn't feel comfortable with, but I felt because of the sources they were coming from, that there would be hurt feelings or anger if I didn't do it the way they wanted.

One of the hardest lessons that I had to learn – and honestly am still learning – is that you know what is best. Trust your instincts; they won't steer you wrong. I had to constantly remind myself that no one knows my kids better than I do. You have known them since day one. Don't doubt your instincts.

Sometimes my babies needed to have a little five-minute cry before they would settle for bed. My daughter napped better on me than in her crib. Picking them up when they cry will NOT spoil them. From three weeks old, my kiddos slept on their tummies. And guess what? They are now healthy 20-month olds. Sometimes they bumped their heads in their cribs when they were smaller, but no, I would not use crib bumpers. These are all decisions that I made despite outside opinions, and my children are healthy and thriving. Trust your instincts. You have them for a reason. Don't go against your gut.

Support System

Your support system can make or break your situation. In my case, my husband took a verbal beating while I was trying to navigate through the highs and lows of my anxiety and depression. We would get into screaming matches over the smallest of things, and later I would not even recall why the fight had begun.

My fight-or-flight instinct was strong, and when the fight instinct was done having its turn, flight took over. I would take to the streets of our neighborhood at all hours of the night, trying to walk off my emotions and pain. I felt helpless and hopeless, and I just wanted my pain to end. I was tired – so tired – of not being able to control myself, of not knowing what to do or how to handle everything, of just not being able to "do it all."

More than once, I debated about just stepping off of the curb and ending it. I saw it as the only way out because during these dark depression spirals. Nothing seemed worth living for – sadly, not even my children. My thoughts were consumed with how much better off they would be without their "crazy" mother, and how much happier my husband would be without his wife screaming at him constantly for reasons that neither he nor I understood.[3]

I remember trying to explain to him once, that when my brain clicked off into rage, it was like a red haze took over my vision and my mind

---

3 If you are experiencing thoughts like this, please know that they are not true and that you should seek emergency medical support immediately. Your mental health is important and should be prioritized.

was no longer my own. Many times back then, even now, though my episodes are much fewer and far between than they were back then, I can't remember what started the fight or what was said during.

You Are Strong

In the midst of my struggles, I felt weak. I needed help. I needed medication. I needed therapy just to help me function on a somewhat regular level. I hated it. I desperately wanted to be normal again, to be how I was before giving birth.

I felt like I was barely functioning through the day-to-day of it all, and that my babies had gotten screwed when they were given me as a mother. I was sure that none of their memories with me would be happy. I was so lost in my own fog that I was sure that I was doing nothing right. And even though most days I wanted to just throw the blankets over my head and hide, I didn't. I got up. I had to, for them. They needed me.

My husband and I recently had a conversation about those days, and he told me that he knew how much I was struggling, but what he saw was me pushing on and soldiering through it all. That shocked me, because I didn't think that anyone could see the effort that I was putting in. He credits me with how good our kiddos are turning out, which makes me feel like maybe I am stronger than I give myself credit for. So you may not feel strong, but someone else sees your strength and is inspired by it. You may not feel it, but it's there. When push comes to shove, you are stronger than you will ever know.

I would love to say that thanks to medication, therapy, and a support system, that I am well on my way to being healed. Sadly, it's not that easy. Healing is a journey, and mine has been filled with more bumps than a school parking lot. But for every two steps back, I continue to push forward, because of my kids. They deserve a healthy and happy mom. Most importantly, they need to know that it's okay to struggle, as long as you don't let it stop you. And because of them, I won't let my struggle stop me.

KERRY GIBSON

AUTHOR PHOTO: MELISSA YVONNE PHOTOGRAPHY
INSTAGRAM: @HONEST.AS.FUCK.MOM
HONESTAFMOM.SQUARE.SITE

CHAPTER 8

My story starts off with a glorious morning: I decided to treat myself to a McDonald's breakfast. Then my husband dropped off a SECOND McDonald's breakfast on the way to his job site. I had double the breakfast burritos and iced coffees. In other words, it was shaping up to be the perfect day. I was driving into work on a high, windows down, music blasting, singing at the top of my lungs. And then, everything went black – literally – and my life changed in ways that I could never have anticipated.

I blacked out, with no warning, while driving 120 km/h on the 401. I somehow managed to pull across 5 lanes and get off the highway, and immediately called my dad to see if he could pick me up. I was scared as hell. When he arrived with my stepmom, the first thing she asked after hugging me was if it was possible that I was pregnant.

Huh?

It turns out, yep, it most definitely was possible.

I'd been pregnant once before – years ago, at a time when I knew without a doubt that I wanted to terminate the pregnancy. I called my mom and she made an appointment for me at a women's clinic in Toronto. After a few days of intense nausea it was all over. I was introspective, but thankful.

This time things felt different. It was like a ghost of that first pregnancy. The symptoms barely noticeable. It wasn't planned, and I wasn't sure I was much closer to being ready for motherhood, but as the days went on I felt myself growing more and more attached to the idea. I downloaded an app, and we gave the embryo a nickname. I found out my brother and his girlfriend were expecting and due about a week before we were. Cousins, so close in age! How perfect!

I fought with the receptionist at my general practitioner's office to get me an appointment within the week, insisting, "I blacked out while driving! There's no way I'm waiting a month to see her."

Then, the ultrasound. Thirty uncomfortable minutes with a tech asking me every question starting with "You're sure…?" but I didn't clue in. I didn't know it normally went differently. And then I was directed to get the results from a walk-in clinic, since my regularly absentee GP was on vacation.

I liked this doctor more than my own. She had kind eyes, asked me questions and listened intently. And then, she rocked my world in six words.

"No heartbeat, consistent with fetal demise."

I assured her that I was fine, and probably smiled awkwardly. I got in my car, logged into an app to see if the bloodwork from the test I'd taken earlier that day came back: it had. My HCG (a pregnancy indicator) had started to drop, which meant that in the grand scheme of things, I was no longer pregnant. I called everyone that we'd excitedly told about the pregnancy before even hearing a heartbeat. I don't remember crying, but I probably did.

The next two weeks were filled with a fun journey into the Ontario healthcare system, which, as a woman, is a journey I affectionately like to call "psychological warfare."

But first, a re-cap. I, having passed out while pregnant, had to fight to see my GP. When I finally did get to see her, she looked at me like I was crazy for going to her so early. I don't know if you've ever been pregnant before, but there isn't exactly a handbook on what you're supposed to do or who you're supposed to see or when you're supposed to do things or see people. For the worriers of the world, for the people who like to check things off a list, this is absolutely maddening and stressful as hell. This was my first foray into the helplessness of being pregnant. Either there's absolutely no answers for what to do or why something is the way that it is, or, there are twenty answers and all of them directly contradict each other.

But, I digress.

Okay so, then, I booked an ultrasound. The tech there was very vague and elusive and told me I had to talk to my doctor about the results. My doctor was *of course* on vacation, so I was told to go to a walk-in clinic to have someone tell me the shitty situation I was in. I saw three different healthcare professionals over the course of about two weeks from the time that I blacked out, but I had to fight to get an appointment with my GP before 12 weeks. If you think about it, it is pure nonsense.

As you can probably imagine, at this point I was starting to really feel like the healthcare system was not on my side. And to make matters worse, my body clearly wasn't either. My hormone levels put me at about 9-10 weeks pregnant at this point, but my little embryo was sized at approximately 7-8 weeks. That incident in the car, or shortly thereafter, was probably around the time that things took a turn. So, why hadn't there been any blood? Why didn't my body alert me to the sad state of affairs going on in my uterus? And, why the fuck couldn't a single doctor take a minute to explain to me what was happening or what I would need to do to move forward with my life?

I took it upon myself to learn everything through Dr. Google. Which brings me to my next sidebar: so many people in your life will tell you not to look things up on the internet if you're unwell, or doctors don't like it when you self-diagnose, blah blah blah. **In my opinion, I think you should do it.** Look up the thing, get your facts straight, have an idea of the steps you need to take to get yourself better because frankly, if you're not going to do it, there aren't a lot of paid professionals that will do it for you.

Yes, that's right; I'm saying that you can't (always) trust medical professionals to have your back. And this is coming from a person who will go to a hairstylist and say things like, "Hmm, I don't know. Whatever you think is best. You're the professional!" So this isn't a control thing. This is a lifetime-of-terrible-healthcare-experiences thing.

Dr. Google, my most knowledgeable and caring healthcare provider at this point in my life, told me that there are a million different ways, words, and medical terms for how a pregnancy loss occurs. What I was dealing with is often referred to as a *missed miscarriage*: the embryo would not carry on in the pregnancy, but my body didn't get the memo. Instead of cleaning things out, it was carefully considering its options: infection, torture, or finally and unexpectedly start the bleeding and cramps, probably at the most inopportune time, like while I was at work.

FUN.

Dr. Google also told me that if I wanted to move on with my life and not be held hostage by the idea of waiting for my body to clear things out itself eventually, I could either take Mifepristone (the "abortion pill" now that it was FINALLY available to women in Canada), or I could get a Dilation and Curettage procedure (D&C, what I had to do when I chose to terminate my first pregnancy). So, I called my GP to find out how to proceed in procuring Mifepristone. They told me that I had to either wait months for a referral to an OBGYN, or go to an emergency department and request it there.

At this point I was obviously thinking, what the fuck? My GP, who has all my information, can't (or won't) prescribe me the pill that I need to avoid infection and potential damage to my uterus, but I can go to a stranger who has absolutely no concept of my medical history and waste valuable hospital resources instead? Okay. Sure. That seems totally reasonable.

My husband was very supportive, but worked for Bell (which is, in my opinion of course, a notoriously terrible employer) and couldn't take time off. So when I told my sister I'd have to go to the hospital to try to procure this mythical miracle drug, she packed a bag and moved in with me for a few days to be there through it all. I was so, so privileged to have had people with me every step of the way; I cannot imagine the additional pain and suffering of the unimaginable number of women who have to go through this when they don't have a strong support system.

The first hospital visit was about six hours and involved a lot of ginger ale and crackers, very kind nurses, and a doctor who was as empathetic as he could be. Unfortunately, I had taken another blood test and somehow my HCG had started to rise again. The doctor was baffled and no longer willing to prescribe me the pill; and, much worse than that, he sent me home with both the hope that the pregnancy was somehow still viable, and the concern that I may have an ectopic pregnancy.

Looking back, I think that if he had properly reviewed the ultrasound information he would have seen that the embryo was in my uterus and wouldn't have left me with such fears. But at the time, I was both excited (there might be a chance!) and terrified (if it was ectopic, my life was in danger). Dr. Google offered me no help that night; there was nothing I could find on HCG dropping and then rising. It was a sleepless night with my thoughts running wild, and allowing myself to think about the possibilities again.

As per the empathetic-but-confused doctor's recommendation, I went back the next day for another painful ultrasound. Then I sat around for about three hours before they took another blood test. Then I sat around until a different, much less giving-a-shit doctor came by to say the ultrasound didn't show a heartbeat but he couldn't explain the HCG rising after dropping, so he called the OBGYN on-call at the nearby hospital and recommended I go there to see him.

I got there by about 2:00 p.m., and sat in various waiting rooms without really seeing anyone until just after 11:00 p.m. Every time I asked if I could get an update or leave to get food because my body still thought I was pregnant so I was starving and nauseous, I was told to sit down and wait and not eat anything. But no one told me why I shouldn't eat anything. At this point, as far as I knew based on what little I'd been told by the doctors I'd seen in the last 24 hours, my little embryo might still be okay.

WELP. When we finally saw a resident doctor just after 11:00 p.m., she really stomped all over that little bubble of growing hope that I had. She blew into the room talking about how I would just have to wait maybe a couple more hours to see the OBGYN, and when I asked again about food she told me I couldn't eat because of the anesthesia.

"Huh?"

"You can't eat because it could cause complications when you're anesthetized."

"What do you mean? What's happening?"

"For your D&C."

"What do you mean for my D&C? We've been waiting all day to see someone because my HCG rose last night and the doctor said the pregnancy might still be viable, and the other doctor we saw today wasn't sure. Are you saying it's not viable?"

Folks, I kid you not – this resident doctor actually giggled. She actually giggled like she thought it was the most preposterous thing I could think that there was a chance. Like she had no fucking idea what kind of tricks my mind was playing with me after another doctor literally told me there was a chance. Like she had no fucking idea that she was giggling about a pregnancy loss. Like she had no fucking idea I was ready to rip her head off.

"It is definitely not viable. There's no heartbeat. So like I said, just stay put and don't eat or drink anything and we'll come get you when we're ready."

Uh, like hell you will. I'm starving, you're the absolute worst human being, and I will not be allowing you to treat me this way, even as a bystander. I'm nauseous, I'm fucking exhausted, and now, thanks to you, I'm the most devastated I've been through this entirely shitty journey.

I mean, that's what I thought to myself. But to her I said: "Um, okay."

And then as soon as she left, we did too. My phone rang at 4:00 a.m. and someone left a voicemail advising me to check in because they would start to prep me for the surgery – thank fucking goodness we left when we did.

The next day, I called my GP *again* and explained the situation. Somehow the result of that conversation was much different than a few days before – no problem! We'll refer you to an OBGYN and you'll be seen shortly. COOOOOL. I was so glad to hear it could have been that simple and we could have cut out the super awful emotional roller coaster ride that was the prior few days.

Two days later, I got to sit in a waiting room filled with baby bumps in various stages just to sit down with an OBGYN who gave me another lovely reality check. He told me that he did not want to prescribe Mifepristone because if it caused hemorrhaging, my best case scenario would be "sitting in the waiting room of an emergency department for at least four hours before being seen by an OBGYN, but worst case scenario, you'll be there for about a day before anyone will be able to help you."

So, I set up an appointment for another D&C in a week. I was told that even with an appointment, the same thing would likely happen where I would likely end up in the waiting room for 12+ hours before they could fit me in for the procedure. In a GTA hospital, probably one of the biggest in Durham Region. I couldn't stop thinking... *What the hell kind of system is this?*

Meanwhile, at this point I had taken just over a week off of work trying to deal with this nightmare of a situation. I had one manager who was very understanding, as she'd been through similar experiences, and another who very clearly was starting to judge what she must have considered to be a lack of work ethic.

I had just signed on for my first management position as a secondment a month before. I worked for an insurance company where executive roles were exclusively male, high-level management roles were exclusively female, and the Unit Manager role was basically a boy's club that I somehow stumbled into out of pure dumb luck.

I was determined to continue proving my value to a company that I truly appreciated working for at the time. I had told the two managers I reported to exactly what was going on with me, thinking that my accidental pregnancy and subsequent loss would not be held against me.

Oops! Big mistake.

I hated the idea of my body suddenly figuring out what was happening while I was at work, but I sensed immediately that I was on thin ice with the manager I worked more closely with, so I started to go into the office again. I sat through every meeting terrified that I would start to feel cramping. I told my managers that I wouldn't be able to make it to their annual employee boat cruise/drunken mess extravaganza, because that was the day that I was supposed to be sitting in a waiting room, hungry, exhausted, and nauseous, hoping to finally be released from the embryo that was holding my body and my mind hostage while it continued to exist inside of me.

I found out months later in a performance review that one of my managers considered that poor form, and thought that I wasn't trying hard to be as engaged with the staff as I should be. I'm not sure why someone would think that I was choosing to forego a fun time with my friends for a day of waiting room bliss, but sure, okay. This one's on me, boss. That was around the time that I realized the company that I worked for was completely full of toxic misogyny, racism, the works.

For years I had pushed down the discomfort that was bubbling inside of me around men I worked with rubbing my shoulders, saying creepy things about my tattoos, and nonstop sexual harassment. There was even one incident where someone, whom I had considered a friend until this point, got brazenly drunk and high at our holiday work gala and proceeded to chase me around the parking lot in front of a bunch of Unit Managers, talking about the super fun things he wanted to do with my breasts. Did anyone tell him off? Nope. In fact, I was told off for talking to him.

Again, I digress. Sort of.

I managed to make it through the week without incident, but hated the idea of waiting all day and night again. I wanted it over with. I called the clinic in Toronto that I had been to once before; they had an appointment first thing Friday morning, and I gladly took it.

It was the most painful, excruciating few minutes of my life. Mentally, things were bad enough. But at this clinic, they provide you with what is the equivalent of strong Advil, and you're wide awake while the procedure is done. I remembered it hurting when I had my abortion there years before, but I do not remember vividly wanting to die. There is no other way to put it. If I wasn't being held down, I can't promise I wouldn't have tried to jump out the window, several stories up. I was loudly chastised by one of the nurses for not breathing through the pain – what the actual fuck? Are you joking?

I'm not trying to steer anyone away from D&C for any reason. I don't think that was necessarily a normal experience, but I do think that it is entirely fucked up that in a relatively metropolitan area, the options are:

> *1) Wait for body to figure things out, or, get infected and end up with long-term damage to uterus;*
>
> *2) take a pill, maybe bleed out in the waiting room if things go wrong;*
>
> *3) sit in a waiting room for a year, hope that someone eventually is able to fit you in for the D&C you were scheduled for;*
>
> *4) or, go to a clinic where you're in and out in 30 minutes, but have to suffer through what feels like someone carving you out from the inside while awake for a few minutes, (and then, if you're really lucky like I was) you get to sit in the recovery area listening to the two or three patients screaming through their agony too while puking.*

Honestly, I'm not sure what I would do if I was ever in a similar position again.

And yet, for some reason, I decided after that that I suddenly desperately wanted a child. It became an absolute obsession and source of heartbreak. I found that I distanced myself from women I loved who were pregnant. I couldn't educate myself enough on ovulation and cycles and everything you can imagine to do with timed intercourse. I went through two OBGYNs before I finally saw one who looked at me for more than a minute and gave me more than a shrug when I asked why I had lost the pregnancy. He listened to my story, asked me a few questions, did a quick ultrasound, and immediately diagnosed me with Polycystic Ovarian Syndrome (PCOS).

I don't want to count the total number of doctors and specialists I had seen through this part of my journey, but it was too many. Too many that didn't have the time, too many that didn't have the give-a-damn left. So I will always be grateful that I finally found the one who figured it out, and immediately put me on medication based on recent studies and didn't just tell me to lose weight.

My year-and-a-half of dealing with infertility was an all-consuming battle, even with a specialist on my team that knew what they were doing. IVF was not an option in my mind; I would not entertain the idea of my hormones being even more messed up, and having to be even more focused on my cycle. I learned things about ovulation, timed intercourse, and the entire reproductive process that literally no one seems to know about, and certainly no one ever taught me. The last two weeks of my cycle became a daily obsession, trying to figure out if my body was telling me I was pregnant with every twitch of my core, every ache of my breasts. Even the first day of my period, which was always light, I could trick myself into thinking it was a positive sign of pregnancy: implantation bleeding.

It never was, and every month I found myself grieving. I could see that my husband was getting tired of me announcing a new possible pregnancy symptom every day, and I began to feel so lonely. Everyone around me seemed to suddenly be giving birth to the cutest freshies I have ever seen, and while I was so happy for them and their journeys, I would be lying if I said it didn't increase my grief at times.

I'd announce to my husband that we were no longer trying. That was it. We weren't meant to have a child and I couldn't do it anymore – and then I would secretly hope that we would accidentally conceive as we had twice in the past. But apparently that's not how science works.

In January of 2020, I felt so untethered by my infertility that I put myself back on birth control. I didn't want to let myself think it was even possible anymore, consequences be damned. But, as usual, I quickly changed my mind and after a week I came to my senses and threw the pack away.

I still remember, as one does when one has to fixate on these things, that I got my period shortly after that on January 29th. I was numb. I didn't grieve, but I did think about how this meant that my fertile window would probably be on Valentine's Day. We had sex on February 12th just in case the window started earlier than expected, and missed out on February 14th because he had to work. I assumed that since we missed that day that it was a done deal. I didn't bother taking a pregnancy test before my expected period for the first time in forever. I waited until four days after I was supposed to get my period, and walked out of the bathroom with disbelief and tears in my eyes and just nodded at my husband.

I called my OB that Monday because I had started spotting, and when I got there the nurse told me that it was too early to be called a pregnancy – and that crushed me. You cannot tell someone who has struggled with infertility that they are not pregnant just because of some ridiculous terminology semantics. That is pure garbage. I left that appointment feeling devastated and confused, and turned to my new GP to fill in the gaps for me until my next OB appointment. Luckily, she empathized with me and hooked me up with some blood tests so I could confirm that my HCG was rising, and I could remind myself that I was, in fact, very pregnant.

I sobbed on the exam table as my OB, a resident, and the oblivious nurse, stood around me and we listened to a faint heartbeat at just over five weeks. Definitely pregnant.

For once, I loved my PCOS belly, which grew absurdly quickly. I laughed off the shitty comments from my mother-in-law ("are you sure you're not having twins?") and a childhood friend on Facebook who was further along and much tinier ("at least you can easily use the with child parking spots!"). I was thrilled that so early on, I had a visible reminder that the embryo became a fetus.

Each milestone we made it past, I became a little more hopeful. I thought I wanted a boy, but I began to dream about a little girl, and cried tears of joy when the ultrasound tech confirmed there was 100% no penis attached to my little growing, super active fetus. I hated her 5:00-7:00 a.m. hiccup sessions that kept me awake, but any morning they were missing I would cry until I felt her kick. It was a hard, beautiful, easy, terrifying pregnancy.

I delivered her after 18 hours of excruciating back labour. It started at 9:30 a.m., was agonizing by 2:00 p.m., and I wasn't allowed to have an epidural until 9:30 p.m. because I hadn't dilated. It didn't seem to matter to anyone that I was sobbing, screaming, and vomiting every 1-2 minutes for hours.

In case you are wondering, there is no breathing away back labour pain. There is no walking around or bouncing on an exercise ball. Your body literally seizes up, and there is no world outside of the pure, unadulterated agony.

Once again, I found that I had to constantly advocate for myself. I knew that my body needed help, and the only reason I got it was because I fought like hell to get it. I dilated all 10 centimeters as soon as I had that beautiful, sweet, miraculous epidural, and the OB looked at my lady parts and commended me on one of the least damaging first deliveries she had ever seen.

My fourth trimester was a haze of antidepressants for postpartum depression, sweet baby snuggles, and marinating in my bodily fluids (leaking breast milk, postpartum night sweats, gross lochia, you name it) and my daughter's fluids (GERD baby). On social media, I shared all of the shit that I was going through and had countless women reaching out to me to share their similar struggles that they felt they couldn't openly talk about.

I began to think about how so many women felt shame about their motherhood struggles. And then, I thought back to the beginning of this journey of mine, in 2018, when I spent a year quietly dealing with pregnancy loss and workplace harassment. I thought about how it was easier for me to completely change career paths and move to a non-profit organization with a small pay cut rather than stay and fight to salvage my career, all because of a short-lived pregnancy. I thought about all of the obstacles I encountered in the healthcare system that seem so normal to so many women, but are so wrong, and add to a woman's pain, shame, and guilt spiral when dealing with pregnancy loss and infertility. I thought about all of the painful things I went through in my pregnancy that were just shrugged off because it would probably go away after 9 months… hopefully.

And I thought about my daughter, and how she would be one-in-a-million to manage to go through life without facing similar shitty circumstances, because as a woman, it's the hand you get dealt.

And I thought, fuck that.

So, one day, when my daughter was about six months old, I started creating designs for baby clothes with ideas rooted in feminism. Things that I wish people thought about more from the start. Encouraging confidence and attitude in girls, not just smiles and being happy, grateful little princesses. I draw on all of the shitty experiences I've gone through in the past few years, and all of the shitty experiences other women have told me about, and all of the shitty experiences we are expected to just graciously accept as our quiet burdens in life, and smile our way through.

This little venture of mine is by no means outrageously popular, or financially sound. But it's my therapy and healing. It's my daughter's future. It's a way to keep connecting with women who haven't found their voice – or are trying to find their voice – in a world that says women need to speak ten times louder, ten times more often, to be heard.

You guys, it's almost as good as two McDonald's breakfasts in one day.

KINDNESS IS
NEVER WASTED. IT BEGINS
WITH UNDERSTANDING
THAT WE ARE ALL
STRUGGLING WITH
SOMETHING.

KRISTA WATSON

AUTHOR PHOTO: KATEY BATTELLE | WANDERSTOCK IMAGES
INSTAGRAM: @KRISTAWATSON123 | CHANGEWITHYLO@GMAIL.COM

CHAPTER 9

Here I am, stronger than ever. At 47, I feel the best that I have ever felt. You see, I didn't always feel this strong, nor did I ever feel great. After battling Crohn's disease and colitis for the better part of my life and feeling like shit literally every day, I didn't know what it was like to feel any other way. I always thought this was the card that I was dealt, so I carried on with life as I knew it.

I'm a proud mother of three amazing children: Rebecca, Steven, and Amanda. I'm married to my soulmate, Darren. My name is Krista, and I am here to give hope and inspire others who may be as desperate as I was in finding better health more naturally.

As I look back over the years of parenting, with Darren and I both running businesses, we had just purchased a farm, with a pet lodge, and soon-to-be horses and chickens. Our busy lives were about to become even busier. Each day felt like it rolled into the next. I didn't know what life could be like without a diseased body. I just tried to do the best that I could to show up for my family.

After my formal diagnosis of Crohn's and colitis in 2012, I was put on Imuran and was on and off prednisone to help keep my symptoms under control until I could have bowel surgery. Much to my surprise, after I was diagnosed, through tests it was discovered that I had so much scar tissue from being untreated for so many years that it had to be removed. I wasn't too keen on having the surgery, however I felt hope that I'd feel better and be able to enjoy more time with my family without always feeling sick and rundown. My hope – along with doctors' – was that they would remove the portion of bowel that was damaged and diseased, and then I would be in remission.

Unfortunately, after only three months post-op, my symptoms came back with a vengeance. I was left with no other choice but to go back onto heavy medications.

Over a couple of years, I was on a few different medications. None of them seemed to help, so I was put on Remicade. I went in every eight weeks for an infusion in which one of the ingredients in it is living rat cells…like what!!! Remicade also had a list a milelong of horrific side effects, with the last one being "may shorten your life expectancy."

I remember thinking at the time – "quality over quantity." How did those words ever come out of my mouth? I guess I was just so desperate to live a "normal" life. My children didn't deserve to see me in pain every day and our busy lives were only getting busier.

Living on such strong medications and not knowing there was any other way to find remission, I kept putting my trust in the medical system. I even sought the advice of many dieticians that were referred by my doctor.

Sadly, looking back now, I can honestly say the advice that was given was only causing more harm. I was just thankful that there was a drug that would help with my symptoms, however I never did find remission during that time.

As time went on, I started experiencing more and more issues with my body. Every joint hurt. I could barely walk up a flight of stairs as the pain was so bad in my knees. I had exhaustion like I have never experienced before. I'd work all day and come home and sleep for hours. I felt like I was struggling to remember simple tasks. Even composing an email had become difficult.

I talked to my gastrologist about my worsening symptoms on a couple of different visits as I was getting concerned. I am not one to complain, so when I do, it's a legitimate concern! My doctors thought that I had drug-induced lupus. Fair enough; I just kept on pushing through each day the best that I could.

It wasn't until the Fall of 2016 when things got extremely concerning with my health. My body was declining so quickly. I had become dizzy and was walking into walls. I was in bed with what I called a "bleeding headache" for three days. During that time, I woke from a nap completely deaf in my right ear. I knew that this was so much more than drug-induced lupus. I saw my family doctor, who was amazing. She booked me for several tests, including a hearing test and an MRI of my head.

As I was waiting for the tests, my health continued to decline. I had started blacking out and speaking gibberish. When I'd come to, I didn't have a clue what I had said, let alone what had happened. I had started dropping items that were being passed to me, and my eyes would just randomly start wondering. I was sleeping most of the day, not able to work any longer. My fine motor skills were declining.

In the pit of my gut, I knew exactly what was going on. I remember one day, standing in front of a mirror, tapping on the side of my head. I kept saying to Darren, "I feel like there is something in there." I think we both thought the same thing, but were terrified to speak the words. It was a waiting game at this point. Fall turned into winter, and we were in the middle of Christmas holidays, still waiting for my MRI.

I finally had my MRI in mid-January, and just like that, our lives were changed with just one sentence. "You have a brain tumour." I was escorted from the MRI table to a room where a radiologist was waiting to speak to me. As the doctor was speaking, I was in a daze, not sure if

I was going to throw up or lose my fucking mind. A fit of rage came over me, nothing like I had ever felt before. For a split second I felt as if I was in a dream, or should I say, a nightmare. However, in that same moment a sense of relief came over me. I finally knew what was wrong with my broken body. With all of my symptoms that were getting worse by day, I finally had a diagnosis. It was the diagnosis that both Darren and I feared the most.

What came next was the hardest thing I had to face in starting this journey. All the way home from the hospital, feeling numb with the news that I had just received, all I could think about was having to tell our children. As a parent, I knew that this news was going to change our three beautiful children in a split second. No matter what the outcome of my brain surgery was going to be, this diagnosis would change our family forever.

When we entered the house, the kiddos and my sister (who had a brain tumour removed 20 years prior) were in the kitchen waiting for us to come in. It was late. This news was sitting heavy on my heart. We had to tell the kids right away; I didn't want to wait until morning. They needed to know and start this uncertain journey with us, from the beginning.

Just days after my diagnosis, I met with a radiologist who was certain the brain tumor was benign (non-cancerous), however it had to be removed. "Big Bertha" was large and was pressing on my spine as well as other nerves. With so many nerves involved, this would explain why I was suddenly deaf in one ear and my eye/hand coordination was so wonky. With the size and placement of the tumour, it had to be removed as soon as possible.

Unfortunately, after the neurologist went over my medical history, it was decided that I had to wait eight weeks after my last Remicade treatment. Being on Remicade lowers one's immune system, so going under a 12-hour brain surgery with an already-weakened body was something the neurologist didn't want to risk. As I left the appointment to go home and prepare for my upcoming surgery, the feeling of numbness was quickly turning into reality.

I slept a lot. I worried about Darren and the burden that was going to be placed on him. He was going to have to run our family business alone, and play the roles of both mom and dad. I worried about how our children were really dealing with what was ahead of us. They were so strong, but I know that the uncertainty of all of this was so hard for them to carry through the day.

The three of them tried to keep life as "normal" as they could. At the time, Rebecca was 20 and about to graduate college, Steven was 18 and just started a fulltime job, and our little Amanda was 12 and in grade 6. All three of our kiddos were at such milestones in their own lives, both Darren and I wanted to see them living as normally as they could while we were dealing with the grown-up stuff.

Darren and I were doing things like getting wills and living wills drawn up, and meeting with lawyers and bankers to get everything in order – just in case. Let me tell you, this is a little PSA: do this shit when you are healthy and not after you get a diagnosis like I did. It's doing difficult adulting stuff that needs to be done that no one wants to talk about, well I just did. Do it!

March 1, 2017 was my surgery date up at Kingston General Hospital in Kingston, Ontario. The team of neurosurgeons that were going to be working on me were the best in our area. My entire family came up to be with me, including my parents. I was so supported from the beginning. I had family, friends, customers, and complete strangers praying for me and my family.

As I was being prepped for surgery, the fear that I had felt leading up to this moment was gone. I felt a sense of strength and calmness come over me. In that moment, I surrendered all of the "what ifs" and my fears to the doctors who were going to give me my life back. It was show time! I was so ready to get this broken body better and to start living again.

As I was getting ready to be wheeled down the hall to the surgery room, I looked at Darren and the kids and said, "I've got this." I had never felt so confident or brave before. I felt so loved and so held. As I was drifting off to sleep for the 12-hour surgery, I was gifted with the most precious nurse. She started asking questions about my kiddos, and as I closed my eyes, she made sure that they were all on my mind as I was about to start the fight of my life.

The surgery was a success! Big Bertha was removed and sent away for pathology, which later came back to be benign (non-cancerous). There was nothing short of a miracle during my surgery. With the concern of Bertha pressing on my spine and so many nerves, I could have been left paralyzed, or suffered brain damage, short term memory loss, or even could have lost more hearing and my eyesight. This was just a portion of the list that the Doctor had mentioned could happen. We knew the risks, but even with the risks, we knew that Bertha had to come out.

We chose to stay as positive as we could leading up to surgery, and we tried our best not to entertain nor speak about the "what ifs." In the weeks before surgery we kept our thoughts, prayers, and energy focused on me coming out of surgery just as I went in – minus Big Bertha!

After a couple of days in ICU and a few more days down in the ward, I was able to go home to finish my healing at our farm with all of my loved ones and fur babies by my side.

The countdown to my next Remicade treatment for my Crohn's disease had started! With all of the medications that I was on, the hospital food, and being eight weeks from my last treatment, I was so excited to know that the time was nearing. My tummy was in rough shape, and I needed to get my Crohn's under control so that my entire body could heal.

Little did I know that what was to come would delay my Remicade treatments for many more months. My fight was just beginning.

Within a few days of being home, I suddenly started to feel liquid dripping from my head onto my shirt. Over a couple of days, the odd drip quickly turned into many, and my shirts were becoming wet. The fluid that was dripping was spinal fluid. It was seeping through my incision.

This unexpected setback turned into many months of uncertainty, and many trips back to the hospital. The doctors were trying everything to stop the CSF (spinal fluid leak) without needing a stent, or another surgery to repair the leak. After many trips back up to the hospital and many failed attempts, I was sent home on complete bed rest to see if that would give the little pinhole in my spine time to heal on its own.

Not long after being home and on bed rest, a pocket of fluid was building up on my neck. The little pinhole on my spine was still leaking but my incision on my head had started to heal, so the fluid had nowhere to go, but to build up between my skull and neck.

As I lay in a hospital bed in our family room, I started to wonder if this was going to be my new reality. Were the doctors going to be able to fix this? What was life going to look like from here?

My hubby made a call to the surgeon to explain what was happening. The doctor felt that with a little more rest, the pinhole would heal and the fluid build-up would dissolve.

Later that same day, the pocket of fluid on my neck ruptured. Never in my life have I experienced a feeling of pain or discomfort like that. It was like someone had popped a water balloon inside of my head. As the fluid gushed out, my brain felt like a dried-up prune. As I was waiting for an ambulance, all I could think about was the worry and new "what ifs" that this would cause Darren and the kids. This was not part of the plan; I was feeling defeated and felt like I didn't have much fight left.

The ambulance arrived and took me to our nearest hospital, where I was then airlifted back to Kingston. The next morning, I was prepped for another surgery to repair the CSF leak. I received a spinal tap so that the path of spinal fluid could be controlled as my new incision healed. OMG, this was more pain like I had never experienced before, even more painful from the first spinal tap that I had received just a few weeks before.

The worsening of my Crohn's disease wasn't helping either. My body didn't have much left to fight with, but I wasn't giving up.

This hospital stay was longer than the others. I was missing home, my kiddos, my hubby, my fur babies, and my life before Bertha. I longed for the hospital visits when Darren and the kids could come up to see me. I know they longed to be with me every day, but that wasn't possible with the distance between our farm and Kingston, our family business, the kids' school, and new jobs.

Thankfully my mama – my rock – never left my side. She spent every day at the hospital with me. She was my ears when I was to "out of it" on pain meds to hear the doctor's daily reports. She was my voice when I couldn't find the words. She was my strength and offered a gentle push when I thought I couldn't take any more. Hell, she even shaved my legs!

As I laid in the hospital, my concern for Darren's health was growing greater. He was under so much stress with everything he was doing to keep things going, including being both Dad and Mom, trying to juggle his time between parenting, the farm, the pet lodge, and seeing me as often as he could, I could see this all taking a toll on him.

My concern for his health really hit me when our oldest daughter sent me a selfie of her and Darren. He looked broken. His skin colour looked off. His eyes were so bloodshot. His cholesterol was high, and I could just see so much pain in his face. I remember looking at the picture thinking "my God, he could have a heart attack."

I had a moment when I thought, *what if something happened to him as well?* I was worried for our kids. No one knew what a "full" recovery would look like for me, and now I was worried about the love of my life having a heart attack.

I knew at that moment that our lives needed to change. I prayed that once I got out of the hospital, that I'd find the strength and the knowledge to make the changes to our lives that we so desperately needed. We were both 300 pounds and were living a lifestyle that was slowly killing us. This was the wakeup call we both needed.

As the weeks turned into months between the treatments for my Crohn's disease, I was in desperate need of help for my stomach. I had finally been released from the hospital to begin my healing journey at home. This journey was very slow and very painful, however we all felt confident that the CSF leak was repaired. I just needed to stay on bed rest for a few more weeks to make sure that things continued to heal.

While in bed resting, I reached out and shared my story on a couple of Crohn's support pages on Facebook. I was hopeful that someone would be able to help me with suggestions on how to get my Crohn's under control until I could have my next treatment.

Paleo and "Clean" Keto diets were both mentioned by several people. To be honest I had no clue what either of those diets were at the time, so I started to do my own research. It seemed simple enough and from what I was reading, many people had a lot of success with both lifestyles.

I was having a hard time looking at this as a "diet." If we were going to make a lifelong change in our way of living, we had to look at this as a lifestyle change, not a diet. Our mindset around food also had to change. Food was not only our fuel; now it was our medicine.

During this time, I also had a very dear friend keep telling me that I should go see a naturopath or an herbalist. I was so scared to do this as I didn't want to have any counter reactions to anything they would give me with the Remicade once I could start that again. She was so persistent and kept telling me, "If you give your body the tools to heal, it will heal itself."

This seemed so crazy to me. My whole life I had relied on pharmaceuticals. That is all I knew and trusted.

With nothing to lose and everything to gain, I reluctantly made an appointment to go see an herbalist. This appointment was like nothing I have ever experienced before. Not only was my appointment 1.5 hours long, the questions I was being asked were shocking. The herbalist was digging into my health right from childhood. Instead of giving me a prescription for my symptoms, he wanted to dig deep into the root cause. This was all so new to me. Without taking my blood he checked my blood?! I know; it seemed crazy to me as well. Who knew that was even possible! Well, it is! I'll save you the details, but it is cool.

It was no surprise that so many of my blood counts were in the black zone. Black, being not-so-good. My liver and my inflammation markers were the worst. Again, this was no surprise to either of us. With being on so many medications during my stays in the hospital, it made sense that my liver had been working in overdrive for many months. It was also clear why my inflammation markers were so high. I knew that my Crohn's was out of control and my body was fighting so hard to heal, but it was fighting from an empty cup.

Before my appointment ended, I was given a few tinctures to take. These would help level things out and begin to fill my cup up again. This was all new to me, but I was willing to try anything at this point. It was after this appointment that I really started looking outside of the Western medicine box and started looking for more natural ways to heal. I'm not saying that there isn't a time and a place for Western medicine; there definitely is and I feel wholeheartedly that it saved my life just a few months before. However, while I was recovering and in a holding pattern until my next treatment, I was willing to give this a try.

It didn't take long until I started to see a positive shift in how I was feeling. My stomach wasn't causing me so much discomfort or upset, and my energy was coming back. I had also seen a difference in Darren's skin tone and that he was also getting more energy. Could this really be from changing our diets and taking tinctures? It had to be. There was nothing else we had changed.

We were 100% committed to this lifestyle change and it was no secret that it was working. Darren and I had been on our new "clean" keto way of living for only a couple of months and I had felt the best I had in years. My Crohn's was under control. I was off all of the pain medications that I had left the hospital with just a couple of months before.

As time went on, the pounds were melting off of us. Within 10 months, Darren and I both had lost 120 pounds. We were like new people! We both looked 20 years younger, and felt the best we had in many years.

With our rapid weight loss, everything I had just been through, and Darren's high cholesterol, our family doctor wanted to follow us closely. She was extremely pleased with our progress. My Crohn's disease was in remission, I was no longer longing for my next treatment after my brain surgery – and I no longer needed it.

After a couple of appointments with my gastrologists, it was decided that I would contact him when I needed to. That was five years ago! Yes, I do know that Crohn's just doesn't go away. My body is still diseased; however, the disease is in remission. Darren's follow up bloodwork looked the best it had in years, and he no longer had high cholesterol. Like, what?! All of this from a lifestyle change! Now, I'll be the first to say that this lifestyle is not for everyone, nor is it sustainable for many, but it worked for us, and it changed our lives.

As little changes were becoming big changes in our family, the next step was to rid our house of nasty chemicals. Prior to my diagnosis of Big Bertha, I had already ditched candles and replaced them with diffusing essential oils. Switching candles was easy for me and that was the extent of my use of oils. Even though the essential oils I was using were therapeutic, I wasn't about to start using them topically or ingesting them. I had the same worry as before with natural remedies counteracting with pharmaceuticals, but now I was no longer on any pharmaceuticals, and I was still seeing positive results with the tinctures I was taking.

What did I have to worry about? My mindset had to shift again. I needed to do research of my own before I started ingesting these essential oils and before I was going to rid our home of all the products I had used my entire life.

I was very saddened to learn just how harmful conventional products are, and I was surprised how most of these items were approved to be sold in stores. Learning what I did made me realize that we were being poisoned in our own home, with the everyday products we purchased thinking they were safe to us.

Over time I switched out all of our household cleaners, laundry soap, beauty products, deodorant, sunscreen, etc. to all plant-based products, with no toxins and our medicine cabinet became filled with essential oils. I started using oils for headaches, tummy aches, tooth pain, cuts, bruises, muscle pain, whenever something came up, we reached for an oil before anything else.

This was so empowering. Not only had we changed our diets, but we had also cleaned up the toxin load in our home. It was beautiful to see these changes start rippling down to our children, and to now see our beautiful new granddaughter being raised without toxins. Knowledge is power and it's never too late to start making changes.

A couple of years into my healing journey, I felt like there was something missing. This healing journey wasn't over yet. There was still healing to do. I started to feel the urge to start working out. I hadn't set foot inside of a gym in over 10 years and I was still experiencing a lot of neck pain and mobility issues from Big Bertha's surgery. The thought of working out made me cringe. I couldn't imagine putting my body through more pain than it was already in. I was comfortable with my daily activity limits, and never thought I would push them. But the urge was so strong, and my gut was telling me to give it a try.

My first experience back at a gym was a group fitness class. I did everything the instructor did (who happens to be a good friend of mine). She understood my limits and showed me a couple of modifications that would work with my mobility issues. I left the class and went home and bawled my eyes out. I felt so strong and confident. I couldn't believe what I had just done.

This was the start of the next leg of my healing journey. From that class on, I have continued to work out 3-5 times a week. My once-so-broken body was coming back to life. The more I did to regain my strength – through diet, toxic chemical detoxing, and exercise – the more I appreciated myself and my body. I am a warrior.

I am thankful every day for the blessings that Bertha has brought me, even on the not-so-good days. I made myself a promise in the hospital five years ago that I would live my life every day as if it were my last. The fight was long, and it was painful, but I was worth the fight, and my family was worth the fight.

Thank you, Bertha. Because of you I love deeper, I hug longer, I reach higher, and I never pass up an opportunity to say, "I love you."

MELINDA MELO

AUTHOR PHOTO: JENNIE ELLIS PHOTOGRAPHY
INSTAGRAM: @AUTHORMELINDAMELO | MELINDAMELO@HOTMAIL.COM

CHAPTER 10

I was one of nine wild and unruly children living in the infested social housing projects of Toronto, Canada, and being raised by a depressed, anxious, and unmedicated paranoid-schizophrenic mother.

I didn't know my childhood was different from other kids' childhoods. I was unaware other children weren't covered in their own human waste, didn't have cockroaches crawling on the walls, or mice rotting in their food and in between their couch cushions. I didn't know they weren't starving, weren't missing school every day, and weren't shuffled from motels to women's shelters constantly. I wondered if other children longed for the love of a mother and father the same way I did. I wished I had been born to an attentive mother, and a father who stayed long enough to know me past birth.

The smell upon entering our crumbling, forsaken apartment was strong enough to blow you backward and send you running outside for fresh air. Inside, the heavy, stinking air sat like weights on our lungs, making us feel like asthmatics without inhalers. The floor was covered in urine-stained clothes, human waste, garbage, and food that had rotted weeks before.

Mom kept the windows covered with comforters and heavy blankets. She'd sit in the darkened living room watching our big, fuzzy television (the kind you left the couch for, to turn the *click-click-click* knob dial). She'd get around with only the glow it provided.

When we turned the lights on, mice scattered and darted in every direction and thousands of skittering cockroaches raced across the walls and counters frantically looking for a new dark place to take shelter. They were in every crevice. My siblings and I pulled them out of each other's ears, off the bottoms of our feet, and when we ate, pulled them out of our food, too. There were so many it made me think that we were guests in *their* home.

Our cement porch had an enclosed storage space that was about four feet tall and three feet wide. The empty, abandoned area was meant for storing garbage – ironic, since I felt like garbage, too. Mom didn't clean and had no use for it, so I claimed it for myself. I pretended it was my home, my place of safety, my dreaming box.

Mom's boyfriends rested their elbows on it, and I could see their knees through the cracks from the inside. The dark green, deteriorating, wooden doors loosely held black metal handles that rattled. It was a brilliant place to hide on the mornings that I refused to go to school. I sat in there quietly, hugging my knees to my chest and chewing my hair like I always did. The sun's rays peeked through the cracks of the doors and across my face, connecting to the core of my being, and warming my body with its embrace. I breathed better in its glow. I wanted the rays to erase the dark shadows from my face so I could become fully radiant like I was in my dreams. Oh, my dreams; real to me even when I was wide awake.

The front door flung open, making me jump. Mom stood on the porch screaming to the wind for me to get into the house immediately. She wanted me to go to school. I didn't say a word and hugged my knees a little tighter. After a few seconds, Mom went back inside. I nervously chewed my hair and picked at my scabs. I pinched the crawling lice that ventured down my nose after snacking on my scalp. I played with scurrying ants and scratched at the peeling paint on the door.

I rarely attended school from kindergarten to grade three. I hated school and avoided being there. When I did attend, the principal usually sent me home because of how bad I smelled. At five years old, I'd wander off school property and travel down the crime-ridden street alone, past our complex, along a gravel pathway, across a large field, over a set of railroad tracks, and through another field to the park where I played by myself.

On the weekends, I'd try to make friends with kids my age whose parents brought a cooler with them; a good sign they'd brought food. I'd continuously ask if they wanted to sit with their parents for a snack, and if I was lucky, they'd say yes, and share with me. I wasn't like the other kids on the park's playground or in the wading pool. I was parentless and alone. Moms and Dads lathered their kids in sunscreen before letting them in the water. My skin was red and sunburned with huge, bubbling, water blisters on my shoulders and back.

One day, a pig-tailed brunette had fallen on the playground and ran crying toward the open arms of her father. I gazed so intently, trying to figure out their relationship. I wanted what I saw between them, but it confused me. His face looked just as pained as hers, as if he had just fallen, too. I purposely fell right after she did, crying out and holding my knee. I scrunched into a ball but kept lifting my head with one eye open to see if her dad had noticed me. Maybe he'd open his arms out for me too. But he never came for me and continued to console his own daughter.

Another time, I remember sitting on the swing set with my bare feet dangling above the dirt below me. I watched, smiling, as the little girl beside me shouted with pure joy, "Do an 'under-doggy' Daddy!" He laughed affectionately, "Again?"

As her father swung her high in the sky I imagined him swinging me, too, feeling like I was halfway to Heaven. I closed my eyes and soared with her in my mind, flying free as a bird above the troubles of my life.

My imagination was abruptly interrupted when he stopped the swing and told her it was time to go home for supper. He smiled at me as he walked away, leaving me alone on my unmoving, rusted swing. I couldn't muster up the courage to ask if I could go home with him to eat. I was really hungry, too.

I dreamed of a father loving me like his own. I wanted to be loved like the girls I saw in the park. I wanted to feel safe. I wanted a dad who picked me up and swung me around while I giggled out of control. I wanted someone to protect me, laugh with me, and who was gentle with his hands. I wanted someone who didn't hurt me, my mom, or my family.

Why didn't I deserve that? What was it about me that made me so unlovable? Was I not cute enough? Was I too loud? Or was I just in the way? I felt invisible.

I continued to gently sway back and forth on my swing, kicking off the ground with my right foot ever so gently. The rhythmic squeak from the rusted metal chain lulled my mind. I leaned my body backward and aimed my feet toward the sky. I daydreamed of a castle nestled amongst buoyant, marshmallow clouds; the place I imagined I lived. Before long, the fantastical world I created came crashing to the ground and once again, I was sitting in the ashes of my dreams. I was such a fool. I jumped off the swing with tears in my eyes and began walking back home to our complex. I would find my way without my father. My dream would die, but I would live.

I wanted to be back in my porch box anyway. When Mom or her boyfriends would get mad or aggressive with me, I'd run there to be left alone. Even in the middle of the night, I'd sit dreaming on the cold cement with my back resting against the red brick wall of our house. I'd look out to the soothing orange glow of the parking lot lights as my aching stomach grumbled like a bullfrog in the night for food. I assumed my familiar position of comfort, resting my tear-stained face against my knees, hugging them close to my chest while I dreamed of being loved, clean, and cared for.

Mom left our housing complex after being brutally beaten by a woman across the parking lot. When her next check from the government came, she crammed her five youngest kids into a taxi, along with her degrading, abusive boyfriend, and headed to a motel. The seven of us spent months crammed into single motel rooms throughout Toronto, hungry and barely clothed.

A month before I turned nine years old, Mom had taken me and my younger sister, Lorraine, out of the room to stand outside. Mom's relative, Steve, and his wife, Lisa, pulled into the parking lot of our motel. *That's strange. I didn't know they were visiting today.* I faintly remember small visits to Steve and Lisa's country home with Lorraine when we were little, but we were always returned back to Mom. *Maybe they'll buy us pizza.*

Mom looked down at me and Lorraine and said, "You girls are going to live with them now," she said, pointing toward their car. "You can't stay here with me anymore. They're going to take you to live with them," she repeated.

I panicked. "Take us? I'm not going anywhere! I'm not going to live with them. I'm staying here with you." Steve and Lisa approached us. "Mom! What did you do? Don't let them take me! I don't want to live with them!" I screamed in horror. Mom didn't want me… again. This was the third time she was giving me away. "I'll be better Mom, I promise! MOM! *Please!* Don't do this! Don't you love me?"

"Yes, I love both of you children," she said calmly.

"Then stop them!" I pleaded. "I don't want to go!"

I grabbed Lorraine's hand and hid her behind Mom's back. I peeked around her waist. Everything felt different. I squeezed my little sister's hand even tighter and pulled her closer to my body. I felt my adrenaline start to bubble inside and my heart began to race. I grabbed a fistfull of Lorraine's shirt and bunched it up tightly behind her back. I was ready to carry her like a baton in a relay. If I heard even a single word out of my relative's mouth that triggered panic, I'd begin my freedom sprint with Lorraine flailing in the wind like a rag doll. They were getting closer. I prepared my body to fight. I had almost nine years of protecting myself. I was stubborn, and I was fast.

I saw a single tear roll down Mom's cheek, and it made my fight to stay with her even stronger. Mom wasn't an affectionate woman, and until that day, I had never even seen her cry. When that tear fell from her face, it shattered my heart. If it hurt her to give me away, then why was she doing it? *I don't understand.* "If you love me, then stop them!" I could barely breathe from screaming so hard and crying. My chest was pumping up and down and my rib cage hurt.

"**HELP ME! MOM!**" I begged. Steve and Lisa reached toward me but I was flailing too hard. "Don't touch me! NO! I'm *not* living with you and I'm *NOT* getting in your car!"

My shirt was up to my neck from them grabbing at me repeatedly and losing their grip. I was red all over my body but was able to get away. I took off sprinting, trying to get a clean getaway.

"Melinda! Be careful of the road!" Lisa yelled. Lorraine couldn't keep up with me even if she tried; she was little and her legs were short. She willingly took Lisa's hand and went to the car. I screamed at Lorraine to get away from the car and ran to try and save her. That's when Steve grabbed me and forcefully put me into the car too. They tried restraining me with a seatbelt, but I had been taught by my older siblings to take it off and jump out of the car. Lisa sat with her legs wrapped around mine and squeezed her arms tightly around my chest, locking my arms.

Steve quickly jumped into the front seat and started the car. I was flailing my body to escape Lisa's grip; biting, kicking, and screaming every profane word I knew, which was a lot. It was a fight for survival and I would not back down. I continued to contort my body to get away from her grip. I was resisting like a captured fish at the end of its line. They were stronger than I was. They had reeled me in, pulled me from the water, and expected me to live on land.

Mom just stood there waving at us.

Steve began to drive away from the motel parking lot. I screamed, red-faced in anguish. They needed to know this was all against my will. I wanted my mom to change her mind. I wanted her to run after me or make some sort of effort to show that she didn't want me to go. But she didn't. My mom and siblings got smaller and smaller as we drove further and further away.

The rage within me exploded and I became an eight-year-old Hulk. I kicked the driver's seat repeatedly. I bashed the back of Steve's head with a loose hand whenever it escaped his wife's restraint. I dug my bony butt into his wife's leg and used my elbow to dig into her side. I was hyperventilating, trying to break free of Lisa's grip so that I could open the door latch and jump out of the car.

Lorraine was used to my tantrums and didn't understand what was happening. She sat there quietly looking out the window toward the sunset off the highway, the most beautiful and distracting display of colour I had ever seen in my life.

Lisa began telling me a story, "A red sky at night is a Sailor's delight. That means it's going to be a beautiful day tomorrow. A red sky in the morning is a Sailor's warning, meaning you can expect bad weather the next day." My little body had given up its fig ht, and my soul had died. The crimson sky had painted Lisa's face red, making her look evil, but I also saw the sun in her eyes. Was she dangerous? Or could I trust her? My eyelids were heavy. Everything felt heavy. My body sank into Lisa's lap as she wrapped me in an embrace and slowly sang, "Jesus Loves Me."

I spent the next seven years with Steve and Lisa before running away at fifteen years old to live with my church youth leaders, who helped plan my escape. After a year with them, I lived with my older sister, Tracy, her husband, and their young daughter for a year as well. At seventeen years old, I was already engaged to an abusive man who told me I'd never amount to more than the shit on his shoes. I was so empty that I believed him.

I was alone. I had built so much distance between my family. I was empty and desperate for healing. I was broken financially and spiritually. I was depressed, anxious, and full of fear, shame, anger, and resentment. I didn't recognize who I was. I committed myself to a recovery program that changed the whole trajectory of my future.

I fell in love with my husband, Mike, during the winter of 2006, and on a beautiful fall day in 2010, we got married. Three years later, in 2013, the dream I had of becoming a mother came true. Twelve short months later, in 2014, we welcomed our second daughter into the world.

I was sure motherhood would somehow heal all of the childhood pain I had suppressed, that the love I felt for Mike would blossom, and that we'd create a family and become happier than ever before. I could hardly wait.

I had pushed my childhood trauma deep within myself, much like loading an explosive shell into a cannon. Becoming a mother, especially to two little girls, lit the cannon's wick aflame and exploded every shard of brokenness I had ever carried into the world for all to see. It was loud. Everyone heard it, everyone saw it, and many people I loved were hurt by it.

The moment that each of our girls exited my body and looked into my eyes, I would have given my life for them. I was their mother and they depended on me for everything. This was my chance to undo all of the wrongs my mother had done toward me. I swore that I'd be the best mom in the world; I'd embrace my children's every need with affection and bathe them in my love. I'd correct their behaviour with patience and understanding and I'd always be gentle. I had no idea what was to come.

I was like a runner at the start of a race. My knees bent, butt in the air, and my hands placed shoulder-width apart on the black tar, ready to sprint into motherhood. I was ready to leave other moms in the dust, maybe even lap them a few times. I was focused straight ahead, grinding my teeth into my mouthguard. But when the man with the gun put his hand in the air and pulled the trigger, I fell flat on my face, skinned my knees and covered my ears. The trigger. I forgot about the trigger.

My girls were not even one and two yet, and my deepest, darkest fears ripped through my mind, replaying the flashbacks of my childhood. These flashbacks of abuse and neglect sent a flaming dagger straight through my heart. The joy I felt as a new mother poured out from my burned and scarred chest. I couldn't stop looking at my innocent little girls and envisioning myself at their age.

Every night I'd wake to the same nightmare, struggling to breathe. I imagined men like a pack of wolves surrounding my girls, and myself gruesomely killing any of them who took a step toward my babies. Every night was a panicked rush to escape locked rooms and dark alleys while trying to keep my girls upright and quiet while I ran. I battled to protect my daughters against evil humans who captured my crying, terrified girls and pulled them just out of my reach. I couldn't trust anyone in my dreams.

I'd wake to the sound of my own scream as my heart raced. I was short of breath. My throat was constricted and sore. I was sweating. I was crying. I pushed the covers off and walked next door to the girls' room to see them sleeping peacefully in their beds. *I can't keep living like this.*

I leaned my back against the hallway wall, taking the only support it had to offer. I looked to the ceiling, where my prayers seemed to be bouncing off lately. With tears pouring out in utter defeat, I slid down the wall to the floor. *God, where are you? This is torture.* I missed my husband and needed him. I couldn't wait for the weekend when he travelled home from work.

Not many people understood my life, and it felt like a burden to share. Mike did his best to try to understand me, but truly, it was impossible. *I* didn't even know who I was.

My relationship with Mike and others I loved was suffering, my mental health was declining, and my babies weren't getting the best version of their mother. I was irritable, depressed, and lonely.

Two babies in twelve months delivered an afterbirth of postpartum depression. That's what the doctor called it, anyway. If the antidepressants she was offering would make me forget my childhood, I was willing to take them. The medicine masked the pain but didn't take away my haunting childhood memories. It frustrated me. I needed to do the hard work, and repair the heart of my inner child. I knew the self-inflicted incision would cause me pain. I didn't want to revisit the life I had tried so hard to hide. I wanted to love myself. I wanted to allow myself to *be* loved. I wanted to heal.

I placed both of my hands on my chest and closed my eyes. I wanted to rip open my calloused heart and rescue the little girl with matted hair and tear-filled eyes. I wanted to strip the layers of darkness from them. I wanted to erase the stories they told.

I heard a gentle whisper in my heart:

She needs to be with you, Melinda.

With my eyes still closed, I envisioned meeting my younger self in a place of solace and rest; a place of healing. I imagined that I stood on the edge of the mountainside, looking out to the world below me. I saw the setting sun in the distance as its rays danced along with my flowing hair, displaying the strands of red beneath. The wildflowers surrounding me were proudly showing off their colours, pointing their faces toward the light that gave them life. I felt the shadows receding as the warm sun kissed my face. The breeze blew like a whisper, making the tail of my dress tickle my toes.

She called out our name. I turned to see her weakened, small frame walking toward me; her hands grazing the tall grass on either side of her. She lowered her head and stopped. Standing in front of me was the eight-year-old girl living within me.

Look up, sweetheart.

Bending at the waist, I placed my soft hands under her small chin, supporting her face. I waited patiently for her to raise her glance from the weeds to my eyes. I couldn't escape her eyes.

I saw her. I saw myself. I saw the pain in her eyes as she cried out for a mother, a father, anyone to love her. I saw her as a baby, crying aloud for anyone to hold and comfort her. She looked at my lips as I spoke softly to her.

Little girl, what happened to you is not your fault. Please, let me hold you.

Tears escaped the corners of her big brown eyes, leaving a clean, wet trail down her dirty cheeks. I explained to her how far I had come in my life and the journey I was still on. I apologized for not taking her with me and for leaving her alone for so many years. I cupped her face and used my thumbs on either side to swipe her tears downward. I grabbed hold of her small hands and whispered,

I'm taking you with me this time. You will never be alone again.

Our journey was about to begin. We stood hand-in-hand together on the edge of the cliff. While it felt freeing to be on top of the world, I knew it would only take a single gust of wind to push us over. I squeezed her hand, assuring her of her safety. If we were to fall, we'd fall together.

My childhood trauma clung to me like a blood-thirsty leech that not only ruined my family for generations but also selfishly drained the best parts of me to stay alive. I made the brave decision to rip it off and say "no more." I've spent years adhering myself to strong women in hopes that they'd lead me. I have drawn from their reservoirs of hope when I felt depleted of it. I've pulled knowledge and wisdom from their words, listened to their advice, and trusted their guidance. They were solid stepping stones in my life and taught me what it meant to be a strong woman.

I know the hardships that I endured as a child were not my fault. The out-of-control behaviours I had were survival skills that kept me safe. Mom passed her generational trauma onto me and it hurt me tremendously. She finally received help in her late fifties and found a medication that helped her function. While I'm thankful for that, I also acknowledge that her decisions, or lack thereof, have caused me great pain.

I love my mother very much. We've worked hard to repair our relationship and talk every day. However, I've had to let go of the impossible expectations I've had of her. She will never fulfill the role I've dreamed of for me or my children and I've accepted that. I can't call her for advice or ask her to bring me soup when I'm sick. She'll never have a licence to drive to see me or her grandchildren. She doesn't know how to play with my kids and can't be left alone with them should an emergency happen. She can't cook for herself, budget her money, live independently, or host a family holiday. I will always grieve for the mother she should have been, while loving her for who she is now. I'll always strive to be what she couldn't be for me.

I'm still figuring out how to parent from the fractured places in my life. For years, I believed that small, lying, thieving, voice that told me I wouldn't be a good mom because mine gave me away. The voice that said I couldn't love my child because I hadn't been taught. The voice saying I wasn't a child worth loving because I was raised in foster care and never adopted.

I've worked relentlessly to repair the heart of my inner child. I have purposefully broken myself into pieces and put my jumbled self back together again. I'm not shiny, new, or whole anymore. I have scars. I'm fragile. I'm sensitive. Many days, it takes everything within me to hold myself together. I see my failings through a magnifying glass and judge myself, especially as a parent, more than ever.

I know there is purpose in my pain. Yes, I am strong and resilient – not because I chose to be, but because I had to be. I refuse to let anyone turn me into someone I don't recognize again.

Mothers, parenting from trauma is hard, but I promise you, there are still embers amongst the ashes that can be turned into a vibrant flame. You can be an amazing parent while being beautifully broken. For me, witnessing men and women beat my mother while I stood there helpless has made me thankful for a husband who loves me purely and is gentle with his words and hands. The nights I cried myself to sleep without my mom or siblings have made me thankful for the privilege I have of kissing my children goodnight. Begging for food and going to sleep starving has made me thankful for every meal I've made that fills my children's bellies. I choose to *see* my children when I look at them. I *feel* their hearts when I hold them close. I connect with their minds and feel the weight of their burdens. I won't be able to catch every tear that falls from their eyes, but I'll die trying, and I might not always know what to do, but I know what not to do.

My heart is full. I am a biological mom, a foster mom, and an adoptive mom. My family continues to grow, and so does my heart. I may walk motherhood with a limp, but I'm determined to raise children who will run without my scars.

Mothers, you are what your children need. Even when you feel you're not enough, your babies see and feel your heart. Your past does not determine your future or define who you are. You are worth your healing. Choose today to stare fear in the face and tell it that it no longer owns you. Let it rear its fangs and lurk in the bushes, but don't be afraid. Stop intrusive thoughts dead in their tracks and align them with the truth. You have a fight within you and a will to thrive. That's enough. Press forward. Lean into that. Love who you are, and who you're becoming.

You're beautiful.
Love, Melinda.

YOUR RELENTLESS
ASCENSION WILL HELP
OTHER WOMEN SEE THAT IT'S
POSSIBLE FOR THEM, TOO.
YOUR RESILIENCE WILL CREATE
A RIPPLE EFFECT, FOR EVEN THE
PEOPLE YOU DIDN'T
HAVE A CLUE WERE PAYING
ATTENTION TO WHAT YOU
DO AFTER A SETBACK.

MONICA FONSECA

AUTHOR PHOTO: MARIANGELICA FORERO | HONEST HUSTLE
INSTAGRAM: @CERVICALCANCERWARRIOR
MONICA@BRITTANYSCHMIDT.CA

CHAPTER 11

It was an ordinary Friday morning. I was working from home, which was something new for me. A pandemic had just been declared two weeks prior and we were in the first Covid lockdown. I loved being out of the office! The energy there was so negative all the time and it was so draining. I welcomed the remote work. It was on a rotating basis for now, but when I was home it was peaceful with no one looking over my shoulder. My phone rang and I thought maybe it was my Work BFF, as we tried to talk whenever we could. Instead, it was my gynecologist calling. This was very unexpected since I had a scheduled appointment booked for a couple of weeks later, for some test results. My heart sank a little bit when I looked at my phone and saw the doctor's name. I knew she was calling with bad news.

After 13 months of tests and procedures, the doctor said she had the results and confirmed it was the double c-word: cervical cancer. At the age of forty, I had cancer. I knew I had been dreading turning forty for a reason. (Not that turning thirty-nine would have changed things!) For some time, I had searched my symptoms on the web, so I was expecting this diagnosis and I could just feel it deep inside. You just know sometimes. It didn't make the news less devastating. I burst into tears as soon as the call ended. How was I, of all people, supposed to get through this?

We're in a lockdown because of covid and now I had to deal with cancer while trying not to catch covid. The three friggin C's, Covid-Cervical-Cancer. FML. This was all on top of my mental health issues, so I thought I was doomed. I have generalized anxiety and social anxiety. (This is what a psychiatrist diagnosed me with after speaking to me for two minutes, but that's a story for another time.) I felt like I could barely get through most days. I never believed in myself, and I live with anxiety and fear taking over my life sometimes. There is no way I would be strong enough to fight this battle.

I knew that I would have an enormous amount of support from my husband, my siblings, and all of my family and friends. My mom lives in Europe and because of the flying restrictions at that time, she couldn't come to be by my side. That was hard, and at times probably harder for her. I'm not a mom, but I know moms have the instinct or need to protect and take care of their kids – and she couldn't. Even knowing that I would have people ready to help me in any way they could, and they believed I could get through it, I was still doubting myself.

A voice inside of me was saying, "Let's do this Monica! It's time to fight and see how strong you really are." While my anxiety was saying, "How the fuck are you supposed to get through this?" Little did I know, I was about to embark on a journey that would change my life.

This all started back in 2017, such a horrible year. My dad passed away and that wasn't easy. I felt many different emotions towards my dad. There were many things that I had to make peace with, but of course, life happens. Things basically went downhill from there.

I started experiencing a lot of pelvic pain. I didn't think anything of it since it was something that happened sporadically. After some time, I decided to start tracking this pain and I noticed that it was happening once every month, and it always came out of nowhere.

Most of the time I was at home when it happened. I would urinate and then BOOM, a shooting pain that would freeze my whole body. It was like a muscle spasm in my pelvis, and it would last anywhere from 5 minutes to a couple of hours. I would drag myself to my couch or bed and lay there until the pain subsided. The pain did eventually start happening while I was at work as well. Somehow, I got through it, and I never told anyone.

Working in a cubicle can be very convenient at times. I was working in the corporate world for a major company and the atmosphere was becoming toxic. Jobs were being outsourced and people were getting fired but not replaced. I was basically writing procedures to train myself out of a job. Every day I wondered if it was my turn. The stress was overwhelming, I was constantly frustrated, people annoyed the fuck out of me, and I was grieving.

In mid-2018, they finally walked me out. It was a relief! That lifted so much weight off of my shoulders. Maybe now I would concentrate on my health. I knew I was way overdue for a Pap smear since I received two reminder letters in the mail, so I should have booked myself an appointment. I found a new job by September, and I still hadn't booked my Pap.

I started feeling worse and that's when I started looking up my symptoms and discovered cervical cancer. I knew Paps were important, and all through my twenties and early thirties I always made sure to get one. I think I would always get my Pap because it was something you had to do. I didn't really think about how it's screening for cervical cancer. Besides, I only ever had one abnormal result so it's not something I thought I had to worry about.

Finally, in early 2019, I went for a Pap smear. It had been four years since my last one. I remember it being very painful. I was basically stabbed so that's part of the reason I didn't want another one and when I received two reminder letters, I just ignored them. The results of my latest exam came back abnormal, and I would have another Pap six months later.

I didn't want to think that it was cancer, but I knew that it was. I had been suffering for so long. I wasn't just having the pelvic spasms. I was spotting after sex, spotting between periods, sex became painful at times, and it felt like I had menstrual cramps 24/7, even when I wasn't on my period. I was always nauseous, tired all the time, and experienced back pain, and hip pain. I read that being on birth control for a very long time can cause cervical cancer, so there was that for me as well.

The second Pap was also abnormal, and I would need to have a Colposcopy Biopsy. I thought it would be a simple procedure. Everything I read about it made it seem like it was quick and easy. The small cut for the biopsy was a piece of cake. The doctor then started burning or scraping bad tissue she could see, and it was excruciating. I don't understand why I didn't receive any freezing; it was so painful. A nurse told me to squeeze her hand and so I did; I squeezed that hand as hard as I could. When I got up, I thought I was going to pass out and the nurse noticed as well so she walked me out of the room and helped me to a chair in the hallway. I was given juice and once I felt stable, I went home.

The results showed that I had precancer and that it was borderline, almost cancer. That's how the doctor put it. The next procedure was a LEEP (basically a bigger biopsy sample) and that was quite the experience. This time they gave me numbing medication so I wouldn't feel anything. The doctor started the procedure and quickly found out she didn't have one of the tools she needed. The nurse ran out of the room to go find what the doctor needed. As we waited, my legs are wide open and the doctor is holding gauze in place in my vagina. The nurse comes back and says she can't find anything. A shipment came in, but they had to look for it. When the nurse leaves, the doctor couldn't stop saying she was so sorry this was happening. All while she is still holding the gauze in place. Then the phone in the room rang and the doctor answered. She lost it on whoever was on the phone and said she had a patient on the table. She decided she couldn't wait anymore, and she came up with a different way to do what she had to do without the specific tool. She might have been more mortified than I was. I didn't show it on the outside, but on the inside, I was laughing hysterically. I felt like I was being punked! It was just the beginning of many funny moments.

The doctor had to numb me again and burned more bad tissue. When the procedure was over, I sat in the hallway for a few minutes to make sure I was okay. Another young woman was waiting to go in and she looked terrified. It didn't help that I had been in the room so long and she knew something was wrong. I explained to her that the colposcopy was way more painful than the LEEP and that it only took so long for me because of the tool situation. As we sat there, someone was delivering the tool to the doctor, so I told her there was nothing for her to worry about.

The result of this procedure is what determined that I did have cancer. I should have never delayed the Pap smear. If I had gone when I should have, the doctors could have treated me before it was cancer.

It took 13 months for the diagnosis; that's a long time and I didn't feel well for a long time before the procedures. I'm pretty sure I already had cancer way before the three-year mark for the Pap. In my opinion, Pap smears should be at least every two years. It's too long of a process to get the diagnosis, so doesn't that mean the tumour grows during all that time? I feel like it's a bunch of men that make guidelines for women's health. So now I constantly tell women to not delay their Pap smear, that everyday counts.

After the dreadful call from my doctor, I started blaming myself since I felt that I could have prevented this. Soon after, I met with all of my oncologists for staging and treatment planning. I was seeing two oncologists an hour away from home. They're two of the best but what a pain it would be to get treatment so far from home. I felt so lost meeting them. I had no idea what to ask and almost all the info thrown at me went right over my head. That could be why most people have someone with them for appointments like this, but covid got in the way.

One of the doctors told me that the HPV vaccine would have prevented cancer from forming[4]. Great; something else I knew nothing

4 Note: according to the CDC, when used preventatively the vaccine for HPV "prevent(s) the infections that most commonly cause cancer." Centers for Disease Control and Prevention. (2020, September 9). *Safety information for HPV vaccine*. Centers for Disease Control and Prevention. Retrieved September 13, 2022, from https://www.cdc.gov/vaccinesafety/vaccines/hpv-vaccine.html

about. The vaccine gets pushed so hard for kids, that I never knew in the province I live in that women up to the age of 45 can and should get the vaccine. So, something else to blame myself for.

They did give me good news; the cancer was still in early stage 2. It was very close to my lymph nodes but hadn't quite spread. I would receive five weeks of chemotherapy and radiation (chemoradiation). Once that was over, I would have brachytherapy (a type of internal radiation). We decided since my hometown has a cancer centre, I was able to get chemo and radiation there. I would go back to them for brachytherapy. Thank God this was the plan.

I met with two other oncologists at my local cancer centre, and they let me know what to expect. There was more planning for the radiation and then I'd be ready to start. During the planning, I had a CT Simulation. The images were analyzed, and I received three tiny tattoos. Markings that I would now have for life. Three dots, one on the lower part of each hip and one on my pelvis. This would help the radiographer to place the radiation exactly to the tumour.

I was terrified on my first day of treatment, mostly because I didn't know what to expect. I learned that chemo was once a week, but it would be a long-ass day. Chemo would last five hours and then I would get radiation right after. Radiation would be five days a week but would only take about 10 minutes.

The first week went fine and then slowly I started feeling different. The second week of chemo was fucking horrible. The nurse did things completely differently, and I felt so sick. She let me sit with no IV fluids for way too long. Thankfully I never had her again. On the way home that day I noticed my skin looked gray and the nausea was horrible. I thought for sure I would throw up, but I didn't. I didn't throw up once during all my treatment! I often came close, but I started taking some anti-nausea meds prescribed to me every four hours which helped. On the chemo days, I would take extra anti-nausea meds along with a bunch of other pills.

I quickly became thankful that I was going through treatment during covid. The best part was my husband being home. He would drive me to treatment and wait in the car until I was done. He was so worried about me but always stayed so strong just so I wouldn't break down. I know it couldn't have been easy to see me sick.

My skin changed to gray, and I looked like death. I started feeling slow. If someone spoke, I felt like I processed what they were saying very slowly. I talked slowly, and I walked slowly. I also couldn't hear well; my ears would ring. My fingertips felt weird, and my head felt like it was full of air or something. It was just weird. I was confused a lot, and I would forget what I was talking about as I was speaking. My memory was non-existent. My oncologist finally said it was "chemo brain." I would say it's like brain fog but so much worse. The funny thing is through all of this, I felt so calm. I had NEVER in my life felt so calm! Where was my anxiety? When was the fear going to creep in? Nothing but calmness. Wow! Was fuck'n chemo brain helping me get through this?!

Of course, all of the love and support were helping as well. I had an amazing husband by my side, and family and friends would bring me food and books. A weekly girl's night on my front porch and then eventually at my friend's backyard oasis also helped push me to fight.

Most importantly, I had God with me which I think was giving me peace of mind. I was reflecting on my life, and all of the things that I still wanted to do. It had been a waste living in fear. There was still time to do everything I wanted to accomplish. I was looking at everything positively and laughed at what I was going through.

There was a day that my friend group chat asked how I was doing or feeling, and I flat out said "my vagina hurts!" It was true but I was trying to be funny, and they said they laughed so much! One even had to explain at work why she burst out laughing! I didn't want to feel down about it all, so the laughter and jokes were great.

The side effects of the radiation were not easy, but I could only talk about it if I laughed about it. I had diarrhea several times a day. All I can say is there's nothing like baking soda and warm water! I would have to get right into the bath with that mixture because my ass hurt so much! I would also squirt the mixture down my butt so it wouldn't burn as I pooped. I swear my ass was raw. It didn't help that I had a day where as soon as I was done with radiation I had to run to the washroom and the toilet paper felt like sandpaper. So, my butt really was raw!

This is when I started to crack. I couldn't take it anymore. I was constantly in discomfort, always sitting in the bathtub, sobbing and thinking this would never end. My husband would ask me to stay strong, that I was so close to the finish line. I didn't give up, but I didn't really have any other choice. The bowel issues lasted a long time but eventually got better. I don't think things will ever be quite the same.

I later found out that this caused PTSD. I was terrified of going to the bathroom or even being far from home and needing a toilet. The last couple of weeks I also started needing to pee constantly but most of the time I really didn't have to pee. Then other times I would have such an urgency to pee and at times it hurt to pee. Thankfully that didn't last long. It's so embarrassing but it was my reality every day. Nights were getting difficult as my body would feel like it was on fire and all I did was sweat. The heat was unbearable, but it was only at night. Things got rough but I made it! I finished the first part of my treatment.

I fucking did it!

Okay, I couldn't get too excited yet as I still had brachytherapy. I could feel anxiety slowly creeping in and the calm feeling was vanishing. My husband drove me to the hospital, and for the whole hour, I was terrified that I would shit my pants. Luckily, I didn't though. Yay me! I had to stay for three days, and two nights. (I made sure to take my own toilet paper.) I checked in for my stay, and the procedure would be first thing the next morning. Anxiety was setting in again and all I could do was cry as I sat in my hospital room alone.

I woke up nervous the next day, and they told me that my covid results weren't back yet. It had been a week. They weren't sure if I could proceed, but eventually, it didn't seem to matter, and I was rolled down to a surgical room. They eventually did receive my negative results. A nurse told me that I'd be receiving spinal anesthesia, and I must have looked like a deer in headlights. She reassured me that it would be fine. The anesthesiologist was very nice. He felt my spine and said that I'm very boney where the needle is supposed to go. He quietly said to me and one of the nurses that he would inject me just a little higher than he was supposed to. Whatever he did, didn't hurt at all and the nurse quickly said it was over. I laid down, and I was out.

Next thing I remember is waking up in recovery. They attached a catheter, and some applicators (tandem) were placed right into my cervix. Throughout the day I would go for an ultrasound or scan and then back down to the surgical room for radiation. I had to lay still, flat on my back, until everything was removed on the last day. I made the mistake of trying to feel what was happening down there. Rods were sticking out of my vagina, or I felt what the applicators were sitting on as they stuck out of me. It felt so barbaric! I was drugged almost the whole time; it was kind of painful for me. I couldn't contact anyone to let them know I was okay, and it was later in the day that a nurse was finally able to connect with my husband. They planned my checkout for the next day.

When it was time to remove the applicators, it was like giving birth to steel rods. Not that I know what giving birth feels like. I was drugged enough that it eased the pain. They also gave me an Ativan, so I wasn't feeling too bad. I was so happy when it was time to leave! I was so exhausted and couldn't wait to sleep.

Eight days later I was back to go through it all over again. This stay seemed different than the first time, more unpleasant. The worst part was removing the applicators. This time I don't think meds were helping because it was very painful, and I really had to push it out. I wish I could forget the whole ordeal. The good news: I was finally done! Treatment was complete and somehow, I got through it!

The hard part was over, or so I thought. I didn't realize that recovery was going to be so much harder than treatment. I'm crying as I write this because I can feel the way I felt at that time. I felt so lost and alone. Most people weren't checking in on me anymore, my husband was back to work, and I was now alone at home for the first time in months. I wasn't sleeping, I had hot flashes and horrible night sweats and changed at least three times a night because I would be drenched.

There were times throughout the day that I would have sweat running down my face and body uncontrollably, just like a scene on *Sex and the City* with Samantha. Hot flashes would come out of nowhere and I still had poison coming out of my body. I felt like I was always crying for no reason, and I felt nervous all the time. I started to fear that my husband would never want to touch me again. Maybe things would feel different. Maybe he would be grossed out by me now. I felt like I was going crazy!

I wasn't, of course. Treatment had killed my ovaries and early menopause had kicked in, so my hormones were all over the place. I was feeling so many different sensations down there. I wanted to have sex, but I was also scared to. It took time for both of us. I felt so messed up. Sometimes I would be horny AF but I was also dry AF. Like WTF? Fucking menopause was causing all sorts of issues and it was all thanks to cancer. FML. The bad thoughts were getting out of control. My anxiety was back in full force. I had to get control back! If I was strong enough to get through treatment, I was strong enough to get through this. I couldn't believe those words were coming out of my mouth.

I decided to start talking to a social worker and I am so glad that I did. She made me realize that I had just gone through trauma, and it sounded like I was experiencing some PTSD. Cancer is a BIG trauma and I had to take it easy on myself. There was no timeline for my recovery. Thinking of no timeline helped me to finally breathe.

After many sessions, I very slowly started feeling like myself again – if not better. I had to have compassion for myself and continue to take one day at a time. Once I started thinking clearly and I felt like I had a grip on things again, so many things changed.

There was an intimate night with my husband where he kissed each one of my dot tattoos, and I instantly started crying. Then he kissed my lips and told me I was beautiful and how much he loves me. I don't think I had ever felt so loved. It was an incredible night that I will never forget.

Then a great friend brought a project into my life all about mindfulness and affirmations which was very therapeutic for me. I was feeling excited again!

I started cutting toxicity out of my life, so I left a job that I hated, and now I have a job that I love. It's a job that I can feel proud of!

Life is different now, or maybe I just look at life differently. I don't waste time on things that I don't care to do. I appreciate all of the little things and don't waste time on anything that I feel is negative. I have come so far and now I genuinely believe the phrase "you are stronger than you think."

Of course, I still encounter challenges and I'm still learning to live with menopause. I'm now 42 and it's not always easy to handle, but it's not always easy being a woman. We always come out on top, though.

I am currently in remission, enjoying life and making many new memories. I'm so thankful to have found an amazing community of women on social media who have also been through cervical cancer. These women are true warriors! I started sharing my story and I try to raise awareness to help others. Women started reaching out to me, thanking me for sharing because they are going through it, or have been through it. They have questions. They're scared, and just need to know what to expect. Sometimes they have questions about a procedure they have coming up. I inform them as much as I can, and I give them a safe space to talk. I tell them that they are not alone, that they are so much stronger than they think, and that they can get through anything. Now when I say those words, I truly believe them!

Cervical cancer is preventable, and I don't want women making the same mistakes that I made. I will continue to raise awareness however I can, so women know how important it is to always...

Take care of down there.

LIFE IS GOING TO PROGRESS WITH NATURAL HIGHS AND LOWS, AND YOU WOULD BE WISE TO REMEMBER THAT THE LOW POINTS DON'T DEFINE YOU.

SANDRA WIND

SANDRA_GORDON@HOTMAIL.COM

CHAPTER 12

Throughout my life, I have had many obstacles. I have always approached things by rising above. When I would get knocked down, I would pick myself back up and move forward.

Since day one I have always been a fighter. When I was born, my mom was very sick and my dad was working and had my sister to care for. I was sent to be with my grandparents as an infant and adapted just fine, but I missed out on some very important bonding time with my parents. I made up for that time once my mom was well again.

If I had to think of a word that I often hear people use to describe me, it would probably be "resilient." I tend to recover quickly from whatever difficult situation I face. As I got older, I started to learn that when I approached the other side of a difficult situation I could learn something from that experience.

I have always had a love for children. As a young child, my mother ran a daycare, so she could stay home with my sister and I before we were both in school full-time. My father was also always involved with the daycare kids, and everyone would be excited to see him come home from work. I remember thinking that is what I wanted for my own family. My friends would often comment on how my parents always spent so much time together and sometimes even ask me why. I remember thinking about this and then realizing that they were each other's best friends and they just enjoyed their time together. This became a goal for me - I wanted to find my true best friend to marry and spend the rest of my life with.

When my husband and I were dating, the conversation about kids came up and we talked about wanting to have a bunch of children. We also talked about my fears of not being able to get pregnant because my cycles had been a disaster right from day one. They caused me to spend a lot of time with numerous doctors, at many hospitals, testing out different medications. I also had a major motor vehicle accident as a young adult that had me doing years of physical rehab, and I have permanent physical issues and chronic pain as a result. I felt like this was another strike against me in pursuing my dream of having a big family. My husband was so supportive right from the start, and would often tell me that we could have no kids or we could have twenty-five kids and he would be happy either way because we would be doing it together.

I truly had found my best friend.

A year after we were married, we were expecting our first child. The pregnancy went well and I had no complications other than the dreaded morning (all day) sickness. We were so excited to become parents and dreamed of what our new life was going to be like. We bought all of the baby things, had a baby shower, got the nursery ready, and anxiously awaited her arrival.

After a very brief time in labour, Kaelyn was born via emergency c-section. She was taken to the Neonatal Intensive Care Unit where she was seizing, unable to breathe on her own, and had no discernible brain activity. After testing, it was determined that the Group B Streptococcus (Group B Strep-GBS) levels in Kaelyn's system were much higher than normal exposure to the infection, which would suggest that she had it before labour began. Kaelyn was with her Aunt and Dad in the NICU until I was out of recovery, and then she was brought to my room on a manual ventilator which was removed shortly after. Kaelyn passed away the following day in her Dad's arms.

Seven months later, we found out that we were expecting again. This was exciting and nerve-wracking given all that we had gone through with Kaelyn. We were referred to a hospital that specialized in high-risk pregnancies, and they were amazing.

We ended up having a healthy little girl three weeks before her due date. Once we knew that she was healthy, we allowed ourselves to be over-the-moon with excitement. It was a very long pregnancy, but once she arrived, I felt like I could breathe again. I truly felt like we were both meant to be parents and we just loved everything about having a baby. We celebrate every milestone – perhaps as a byproduct of losing Kaelyn or as a result of the pure happiness and joy we experience with Emily.

When our daughter was nine months old, I had surgery on my mouth and sinus to have a lump removed. I had experienced these types of things before and they always came back benign – well, until now. This particular biopsy came back showing that I had lymphoma and required that I start chemotherapy a week after I got the diagnosis. One of our questions for the doctor was about whether I would be able to have anymore kids. They referred us to a fertility clinic.

The clinic told us that the type of chemotherapy I was having was very intense and could potentially kill off my egg supply. They gave us some options and, in the end, we decided that making it through treatment was the biggest concern and we would handle anything else as it came up, just like we always had.

Six months of doing chemotherapy while having a baby at home was difficult. There are some days I do not even remember. What I do remember is that I had the most amazing support system with our friends and family constantly there to help. They were supporting us with our daughter, taking me to appointments, and cheering me up every step of the way. I quickly realized that being positive and looking for the good in any situation could make such a difference.

During the pandemic, my husband and I were fortunate enough to find out that we were expecting another baby! We were so shocked as we had been to a fertility clinic a few years after chemo due to my cycle not returning and us wanting to continue to grow our family. We were told that my egg supply was too low and I was entering menopause, so to find out a few years later that I was pregnant was just amazing.

Unfortunately, we lost the baby very early on. Our hope was crushed. This is when I realized that I needed to seek outside help to start talking about all of the struggles I had faced. I wanted to stay positive but I was also feeling so defeated.

Having this miscarriage helped me to make the decision to close the daycare I had been running and start the next chapter in my life. I had always found peace with a house full of little kids and being able to take care of them but now the idea of having all the young ones return once the stay-at-home orders were lifted from the pandemic had me panicked and completely unsure. This was a big factor in closing the daycare. I had run a home daycare for years while my daughter was young.

How did I decide to start a daycare? I was recovering from a major accident and exploring a new career path. I also wanted my daughter to be able to stay home and not have to go to daycare. Let's be honest, I did not want to miss a thing.

Once she was in school full-time, I was so lost. I was attached to the kids I was watching but also felt like I was supposed to do more.

After talking with a friend I went to college with, we came up with an idea to start up our own business, *Simply Organized with Sandra and Amanda*. We could make our own hours, be there for our families, and do something that we loved. Organizing, cleaning, and helping others has been a lifelong passion for me. The company started part-time while I was still with the daycare kids. Then the pandemic hit. Everyone went into hiding and all of the sudden I was not working at all. As things slowly started to open up again, I was faced with a hard decision. Take the kids back and keep Simply Organized part-time, or take the plunge and try to get Simply Organized off the ground.

I took the plunge!

Due to the restrictions still in place from the pandemic, I virtually said goodbye to all of "my kids" and kept looking after two before and after school kids that I had had for years.

Simply Organized went full-time during a pandemic. I was terrified as there was so much unknown. As much as I miss a house full of kids, it was the best thing I could have done for myself. I often have a hard time putting myself first and I always want to please everyone else. Starting and running this company with one of my best friends has brought a lot of joy to what can be a difficult endeavour. Taking on the challenge of running a business, I have learned the importance of sometimes having to put myself first.

My daughter is now eight years old, and I feel fortunate that my husband and I have a lot of time and attention to devote to her and help her navigate this crazy world we live in. I sometimes struggle with not being able to provide her with a sibling to grow up beside. The beginning of the pandemic was a huge struggle for everyone, and my daughter really missed having all the daycare kids around her. We have worked very hard to help her understand her feelings, learn how to acknowledge them, talk about her sister, and celebrate every beautiful moment with the people we love. I hope that one day, my daughter looks back on growing up and is not sad about not having a sibling to share her experiences with, but instead enjoys the memories we made as a family.

After going through all of these major life events in such a short time, I have had people ask me how I am still happy. I honestly do not know how I could be anything else. I am so fortunate to have the most supportive husband and amazing daughter, and I love the life that we have created. Some days, it takes effort to find the positives, but my mindset is focused on looking for those things – it is always worth it.

I remember a conversation with my husband where we made a conscious decision to not allow what we had been through to define us as individuals or a couple. We had to continue to write our story together as a family. We needed to learn how to let grief and happiness coexist. We did not want to stay in the sadness all the time. Don't get me wrong, I have sadness in my heart that I carry with me daily. I had to accept it for what it is and I realize that acceptance is an active process. I accept my circumstances and do what I can to make them better. I also found that seeking professional help and having someone outside of my comfort bubble is very beneficial. It forces me to sit down and think about the things that I have been through, and to process everything.

I absolutely feel pain when my first daughter's birthday rolls around or the first day of school comes each year. I also feel it when I see another child the same age as she would have been, or someone asks me how many children I have, and the list goes on. It happens all the time. My daughter missed out on creating so many memories because she did not get a chance to live or experience the love that we had to give to her. We did not get a chance to create memories with her.

I have learned to take that pain and turn it into power. I use it to educate others and maybe help save another family from experiencing the heartache we hold. We use her name and spread kindness, love, and knowledge. We spread the word about advocating for yourself with health care professionals, asking questions, and doing your own research. We spread knowledge about Group B Strep and the number of babies that have died or become seriously ill from it. We also spread love by doing good deeds with her in mind, like collecting and donating books annually in her honour, and just being there when someone is in need.

Kindness is never wasted. It begins with understanding that we are all struggling with something. Be patient with those around you – and with yourself. The struggle that you are facing today was put in front of you to help you develop your strength for tomorrow.

Make the choice to rise above whatever your situation is – and find happiness in it.

COURTNEY ST CROIX

AUTHOR PHOTO: HONEY HOUSE PHOTOGRAPHY
@LEADHERPUBLISHING | LEADHERPUBLISHING.COM

PUBLISHER'S NOTE

Ris-ing / /rīziNG/
Adjective
"going up, increasing, or sloping upward."[5]
"advancing, ascending, or mounting"[6]

I think we all have a general goal of rising in life; improving, advancing, growing, evolving… at least I do. Moving forward (or upward) is the generally accepted, agreed-upon, coveted route that most humans desire to follow. I've spent many years of my life focused on witnessing the needle move in my favor (upwards) as my own personal key performance indicator: *Am I better than I was yesterday? Last year?*

---

5 Oxford English Dictionary. **"Rising". OED Online. Oxford University Press, June 2022**.
6 https://www.dictionary.com/browse/rising

Have I made small progress in at least some ways? Am I advancing? What's my next level? How do I get there?

While this can be a relatively healthy way to approach life (reach for the stars!), it stands to reason that life will inevitably throw you some rogue, dangerous and difficult waves. The needle stops moving, or goes backwards. One step forward, two steps back. The peak begins to slope into a downward spiral. When that happens…it will be way easier to succumb to the sinking when the momentum of the tide is already pulling you under.

In order to rise, we must begin somewhere. And sometimes, the only way we can rise is by heading down the mountain first.

It's a universal truth: life is full of ups and downs.
Ebbs and flows.
High and low tides.
Peaks and valleys.
Light and darkness.
Planting and harvesting.

"**For every action, there is an equal and opposite reaction**." This is Newton's Third Law of Motion, and it sums up the law of polarity perfectly. It means that forces come in pairs: negative and positive, action and reaction, masculine and feminine.[7]

Without the darkness, we would be less inclined to understand the light. (Plus, as humans we really do like to compare things, so it makes sense that our hardships would help us appreciate our successes. You know, once we've moved through them.)

As you've now seen throughout the stories shared inside *Women Rising*, we women are fucking *resilient*. It's clear that we can – as Glennon Doyle says, "do hard things" – and often wind up building strength and resilience through challenging and difficult situations, even though it doesn't feel like it at the time. The darkness helps us shine.

---

7 Robbins, Tony. 2022, *The Law of Polarity*. 07/15/2022. tony-robbins.com. <https://www.tonyrobbins.com/ask-tony/polarity/#:~:text=%E2%80%9CFor%20every%20action%2C%20there%20is,and%20reaction%2C%20masculine%20and%20feminine.>

When you're standing nose to nose with a painting, you really cannot see what's going on. It's only when you create space between yourself and the canvas that you can truly appreciate what you see. After all, in calm waters, things reflect most clearly.

This is how you rise.

Life is going to progress with natural highs and lows, and you would be wise to remember that the low points don't define you. (For what it's worth, the high points don't define you, either; we're all fluid, flexible creatures and we all experience our own life stressors in different ways. You are just as valuable, loved, and worthy at every stage.)

I hope that the stories you've read inside this book have helped you to see that you are not alone in experiencing various challenges in your life, and that you *do* have the power to rise above afterwards. That power is always inside you, and it's always available to you. It lives in you.

But, if ever you feel like you don't have the strength required to rise…
When life is knocking you down and you don't know how to get back up…
When a wave crashes over you and pushes you back to the shore…
Grab hold of this book and remember that **you are not alone.**
You are a woman rising.
You are capable of big challenges and hard circumstances.
You *can* rise above whatever life throws at you…

And your relentless ascension will help other women see that it's possible for them, too. Your resilience will create a ripple effect, for even the people you didn't have a clue were paying attention to what you do after a setback.

Thank you for being here, in this space, holding this book in your hands. The women who have contributed to this book have overcome huge challenges in order to have their words published publicly, and I want you to know that your support means **everything** to them.

It's not easy to write a book. It's not easy to peel back the layers of difficult life experiences and learn to heal through communicating your trauma. It requires a certain level of courage and bravery in order to share in this way, and I'm so proud of every single woman who has tested her writing skills and her commitment to show up for others through writing this book.

We wrote this book for you, the one holding it in your hands right now. If you felt something, *anything*, through any of the chapters featured inside this anthology, I encourage you to reach out and connect with the author of the chapter, and tell her how powerful her words were for you.

We are honoured to have collaborated on such a powerful project, and I know I speak for all authors inside these pages when I say: thank you for reading.

And if you have a fire inside that's waiting to be unleashed... stay tuned for future collaborative books that may pique your interest.

Thank you for reading.

Now go rise above whatever challenge is staring you in the face right now.

You can handle it, rising woman.

"Rise above your circumstances, change the world one person at a time starting with you, and be the inspiration you've been searching for."
-Lindsay Stirling

Courtney St Croix
CEO, LeadHer Publishing
Leadherpublishing.com
@leadherpublishing

Printed in Canada

little BLUE HOUSE

www.littlebluehouse.com

IN ORDER TO RISE,
WE MUST BEGIN
SOMEWHERE. AND
SOMETIMES, THE ONLY
WAY WE CAN RISE
IS BY HEADING DOWN
THE MOUNTAIN FIRST.

leadHer
PUBLISHING

To find out more about LeadHer Publishing's books,
services, and collaborative projects,
visit leadherpublishing.com

Manufactured by Amazon.ca
Bolton, ON

31220759R00090